mark Littleton

Beefin' Up

Daily feed
for Amazing Grazing

MULTNOMAH
Portland, Oregon

Cover design by Bruce DeRoos.
Illustrations by Krieg Barrie

BEEFIN' UP
© 1989 by Mark R. Littleton
Published by Multnomah Press
Portland, Oregon 97266

Multnomah Press is a ministry of Multnomah School of the Bible, 8435 N.E. Glisan Street, Portland, Oregon 97220.

Printed in the United States of America.

Library of Congress Cataloging-in-Publication Data

Littleton, Mark R., 1950-
    Beefin' up : daily feed for amazing grazing / Mark R. Littleton.
        p.   cm.
    Includes bibliographical references.
    Summary: An eight-week daily devotional book for teenagers, covering such areas as dishonesty, temptation, control, and popularity.
        ISBN 0-88070-317-2
    1. Teenagers—Prayer-books and devotions—English. [1. Prayer books and devotions. 2. Christian life.] I. Title.
BV4850.L58 1990
242'.2—dc20   89-29297
                                                                           CIP
                                                                           AC
    90 91 92 93 94 95 96 97 98 - 10 9 8 7 6 5 4 3 2

To

Becky and Chris
Steve and Diane

family who make life worth living

CONTENTS

UTTER TRUTH

All right, that title's a bit corny—I'll admit that up front. But we all need a little corn now and then. What we have to find in it is that one kernel of truth to take back to the farm with us.

Just the same, the issues aren't corny at all. In this book we'll look at a number of important elements of Christian living: how to stand up against peer pressure, how to resist temptation, what it means to endure in the Christian life, what's important in this life.

None of these are matters we want to take lightly—and all of us could use a little beefin' up in them.

Recently, I had the opportunity to watch two different groups engaging in body building. One was a women's aerobic dancing class. Talking about "getting down to it!" Those women did. I mean, they were working out, jumping around, dancing through, and holding up like no one I ever saw. Just watching them made me tired.

The other was a guys' basketball game. Now these fellows were serious. Lots of grunting, pushing, knocking around, and sore ankles there. Before the end of five minutes I had had it. I was ready to be carried away on a dogsled.

Both these groups recognized the need to beef up physically.

We Christians likewise all understand the need to get into spiritual shape. But too often we think spiritual fitness is far different from physical fitness. It's not.

Physical fitness takes
    work
    sweat

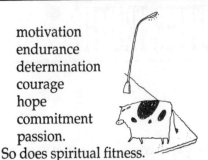

motivation
endurance
determination
courage
hope
commitment
passion.

So does spiritual fitness.

The only difference is the tools you use. In the physical realm, it's your body, a solid regimen, and the appropriate playing equipment. In the spiritual realm, it's your heart, soul, mind, and might. But it also requires a regimen and the right playing equipment.

What's the equipment?

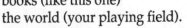

prayer
the Bible
God's people
books (like this one)
the world (your playing field).

And the regimen?

That's where most of us flake off. But the utter truth lying at the base of all of it is this: no radiance without obedience. Or put another way: no pain, no gain.

The Christian life revolves around the issue of obedience. The question is, how much of the word of God are you willing to put into practice and apply to your circumstances? We'll look at that a lot in this book.

But not without a few smiles along the way.

I hope you'll take this book both seriously and in stride—step by step. Every journey begins with the first step. Every devotion begins with the first verse, the first prayer, or the first application. Any way you cut it, beefin' up as a Christian is work. But it's work that can be fun, exhilarating, challenging, and life-changing.

And that's no bull!

WEEK ONE

The Lust for Greener Grass

MONDAY

The Boy Who Wanted a Little Bit of Everything

A Fable

Ralph Pyle was a busy guy. He didn't want much. He didn't expect a lot. Not the head cheerleader as his girlfriend, or the lead role in the junior-senior play, or a '90 Corvette. But he did want a little bit of everything. Just a taste. Just enough to know he'd been there.

When he was sixteen years old, he went to God and asked him to hear his prayer. Granted, he was young. But you have to start somewhere. And God consented. Ralph said, "Lord, I know I don't deserve much. And I don't expect a lot. But I would like some things. Just a little bit. This is my request: I'd like my own bedroom away from my brother, some nice furniture, a stocked refrigerator, a 110-watt stereo, a girlfriend with looks, and my driver's license."

God understood a person wanting something in this world, so he answered Ralph's prayer. Ralph's parents gave him his own room with a little refrig. He got his driver's license. And then one of the prettiest girls in the school band fell in love with him. Also, he received two pairs of designer jeans, a color TV, a stereo (not the top of the line, mind you, but square in the middle), a record collection, and a boom box for the beach. It wasn't the American Dream, but it was comfortable. Ralph was pleased.

Grazing

This story functions as a fable. It teaches a point or principle. But let's take a closer look. What do you think of

Ralph? Is he asking too much? What does the Bible have to say about wanting things? Is it good or bad?

Let me remind you of two sayings of Jesus. The first is found in Luke 12:15: "Beware, and be on your guard against every form of greed; for not even when one has an abundance does his life consist of his possessions." Note that word *beware*. It's a caution—better take a second look when it comes to things . . . that stereo you want or that sports car or even that new outfit.

The second saying is found in Matthew 6:32-33. After talking about worry and anxiety over basic needs—food and clothing—Jesus concludes, "For all these things the Gentiles eagerly seek; for your heavenly Father knows that you need all these things. But *seek first His kingdom and His righteousness* [my emphasis]; and all these things shall be added to you." When we put the right things first, God provides the secondary things.

Still, Ralph's a fairly normal guy, isn't he? It's not wrong to want to have nice things. You just have to keep it all in perspective.

When I was growing up, our next-door neighbors' Christmas was the talk of the family. Every year we always wanted to go by their house and see the horde of gifts they'd collected. It was monstrous. Always the latest gadgetry—robots, dolls that talked, you name it. They had what I could only dream about.

But one thing I always noticed. They seemed to have the worst fights I'd ever witnessed—and over such trivia.

"You can't play with that—it's mine!"

"You didn't give me such-and-such so I'm going to scream my head off until I get it."

Things.

They can tear our guts out. We want them when we want them how we want them. And not any other way, thank you!

This focus can turn you into an eternal brat.

How do you see it? Can you "seek first His kingdom," knowing all the rest will come from God? Or are you obsessed with the stuff down here?

Chew for Thought

1. Read Matthew 6:19-24 and 25-34. What do these passages say about "things" to you? _____
_____
_____

2. What "things" are most important to you? Why? List them and try to imagine living without them. How would you feel? _____
_____
_____

TUESDAY

Wanting to Call the shots

Nonetheless, about a year after living in the lap of mediocrity, Ralph Pyle suddenly decided he still wasn't satisfied. "Everyone's always telling me what to do. My mom. The teachers. My brother. My sister. For once, I'd like to call some of the shots."

He again told God what he wanted. God listened and asked, "What kind of shots do you want to call? Do you want more freedom, no one telling you what to do, a place in student government?"

"That's it," said Ralph. "A little bit of all of the above."

God answered quickly. Within a month, Ralph was signed up to vote on a special youth board at his church. He was also asked to represent the student body at the local PTA meetings. He was nominated for treasurer of his class. He became co-captain of the soccer team and got a job as a trainer at a local Burger King with two sophomores under him.

Ralph was happy. He knew he wasn't a particularly ambitious guy, not like some of the guys he met. They went to school early, came home late, and never seemed to get a moment's rest. But Ralph took naps. His parents listened to him. The dog sat when he said, "Sit." The kids on the youth board listened to his advice. His class liked him. The soccer team did well under his leadership. He was very happy.

Grazing

For some people, getting a position on the yearbook staff, on the swim team, or in student government can seem like the end-all of existence.

Jesus said, "You know that the rulers of the Gentiles lord it over them, and their great men exercise authority over them. It is not so among you, but whoever wishes to become great among you shall be your servant, and whoever wishes to be first among you shall be your slave" (Matthew 20:25-27).

The right to call the shots, to be your own person, to have more freedom, to be "in charge" can be a powerful tool. But what happens once you get there?

Chuck Colson is one who has tasted the place of influence. In the ill-fated Nixon administration he held the position of one of Richard Nixon's closest advisers. He was known as the "Hatchet man" because of his strong-minded ability to deal with the tough problems. But all that began to fade after the election of 1972. The night of the voting returns, it was clear that Nixon had tromped George McGovern. Colson, Nixon, and another aide, Bob Haldeman, were in the White House watching the returns. It wasn't a happy victory. Watergate (the scandal that would eventually topple the Nixon administration) had begun to break wide open.

Haldeman sat hunched over a table angrily totaling up election figures. Colson was drinking himself drunk. And Nixon kept rejecting drafts of the telegram he would send to his opponent. He couldn't find anything to say that was gracious but unfriendly. Colson writes, "If someone had peered in on us that night from some imaginary peephole in the ceiling of the President's office, what a curious sight it would have been: a victorious President, grumbling over words he would grudgingly say to his fallen foe; his chief of staff angry, surly, and snarling; and the architect of his political strategy sitting in a numbed stupor. Yes, the picture was out of focus. If this was victory, what might these three men have looked like in defeat?"[1]

Remember—I'm not knocking the desire to be first or in charge. We need to be involved. Many have good reasons for their need to lead. And some of us should lead the rest. But when it becomes your passion, the only thing you think about, what then?

Chew for Thought

1. Read about a person who called the shots in Luke 12:13-21. Where did he end up?_____
_____
_____

2. Do you want to be in charge? Why do you think God puts people in authority—us, and others over us? What good is it?_____
_____
_____

Just a bit of Popularity

But as always, the day came when Ralph sensed something else was missing. He was seventeen now and a senior. He began to realize a little bit of money and power wasn't all it was cranked up to be. He contemplated his problem and suddenly he realized, "No one knows who I am, except, of course, my parents and a few of the locals. I think if I had a little taste of real popularity, just a little piece of it, I would be happy." Again, he talked with God about it. At first God didn't understand. "I know who you are," he said.

"But this is different," Ralph said. "I'd like to have my own car to bomb around in and stir things up. I'd like to make the baseball team and be one of the big hitters, making a headline or two. I'd like to go to the dances and have a lot of girls want to dance with me."

The next few months Ralph had the time of his life. One day he was walking along the street with his dog, and a Channel 11 news truck stopped and a reporter interviewed him about a community problem. He didn't know a lot about it but he knew a little bit, and he told the reporter what he knew. He was on TV that night. The reporter even said, "You've given me some good quotes."

Later, his picture was in the paper when he received an award for most valuable player on the baseball team. His girlfriend cut it out and put it in her scrapbook. At the dance, he got up to the mike and sang a song that had some of the girls swooning. And after working nearly a year at the burger joint, he bought his own car—called it the "Nightfighter," and tore up the street with it.

People began to take note of Ralph Pyle. Not many people, but a few. Just enough to give Ralph a taste. Even

Mrs. Hobson greeted him at the market, saying, "Why, I saw your picture in the paper, Ralphie boy."

"It wasn't such a good photo."

"Oh, I thought it was most handsome. It's not everyone who gets his picture in the paper."

And Mrs. Hobson had even fired him when he was younger for not cutting her lawn properly. It felt good to have her congratulate him.

Grazing

Many people are convinced that meaning in life comes from being famous or popular. But then there are those who discovered that the limelight could become the lemonlight.

Many of the stories are funny. There's one about Lee Trevino, the famous golf pro. He autographed a five-dollar bill one day for a woman during a golf tour. She gushed that she would keep it for the rest of her life. Half an hour later, he bought some drinks, gave the bartender a twenty, and got his autographed bill back with the change!

Ringo Starr of the Beatles was asked how long the mania would last and what they would do when it ended. He said unemotionally, "When it's over and done with, I imagine we'll have nothing to do but sit on the deck of our yacht—and sulk."

But what does the Bible say about popularity? The Pharisees loved having the best seats in the synagogues, and being called "Rabbi" by the people, and being respected. But Jesus cursed them and their attitudes, saying, "Woe to you scribes and Pharisees, hypocrites."

Fame and popularity can become the passion of your life—until you have them. Then you only want more and more. And when more doesn't come, you can end up bitter and disillusioned.

Chew for Thought

1. Read Matthew 23 for Jesus' words about the Pharisees and how they loved being popular and respected. If Jesus were to make a comment about you and your life, what would you want him to say? Write it out below.

_____

_____

_____

2. If you died today, what do you think people close to you would remember you for? What would you like them to remember you for?_____

_____

_____

THURSDAY

Peace

Ralph was getting close to eighteen now and he realized something remained wrong. "I have a little bit of money, power, and fame. But something's missing."

He thought for nearly a month. Then he observed some religious folks who didn't seem to have a care in the world. "Peace," he said. "I lack internal peace."

"Lord," he said, "I'd like some peace. Peace of mind. Peace of heart. But I don't want it to the point where I have to start telling people about sin and such. I don't want to be a fanatic. But I would like a little peace. Not a lot. Not much. Just a taste."

God sat a long time before saying a word. Finally, he sighed. "Ralph Pyle, you have asked a hard thing. But there have been many who wanted such peace and, as always, I've done my best. What you want, I suppose, is to feel good about yourself, correct?"

Ralph nodded. "That's it. That's it. You put it so well."

God was dismayed, but he waved Ralph away, saying, "Go your way. I will send you such peace."

No prayer was ever answered so quickly. That week, Ralph went to a positive self-image seminar. Afterwards, he felt so good, he took his girlfriend out to dinner.

A few weeks later, he listened to some tapes by a famous television preacher. Soon, he was so positive and inspired, his family wondered what had happened. Finally, he bought some books about guilt. After learning the formulas and applying a few of them, he felt such relief he nearly walked on air.

Grazing

Having a strong self-image is an important ingredient in healthy living. But often a person has to feel bad about himself or herself before he or she can feel good. Self-image is not just related to good feelings, but also to faith, forgiveness, hope, and a sense of meaning in life. What Ralph wanted was "good internal vibes." But is that what we really need?

What is the nature of real peace? Perhaps Paul's words in Romans 5:1-2 capture the idea best. He said, "Therefore having been justified by faith, we have peace with God through our Lord Jesus Christ, through whom also we have obtained our introduction by faith into this grace in which we stand; and we exult in hope of the glory of God."

Self-esteem is enjoying being who God made you to be.

Norman Rockwell was a famed illustrator throughout most of the twentieth century. But at one time he was struggling to make his first major sale. One of the best markets he could go after was *The Saturday Evening Post*, but its editor was a tough old bird named Lorimer. Rockwell hadn't sold him anything. In fact, he hadn't even tried. His friend Clyde told him to put something together and show it to the *Post*. Rockwell drew a portrait of a sensual couple in an embrace, a kind of cover that was popularized at that time by another illustrator named Gibson. Norman did another one of a ballerina curtsying under a spotlight. Then he showed them to his friend Clyde.

Clyde wasn't pleased. He said, "You can't do a beautiful, seductive woman. She looks like a tomboy who's been scrubbed with a rough washcloth and pinned into a new dress by her mother. Give it up." He picked up a recent *Boy's Life* cover Norman had done and said, "Do that. Do what you're best at. Kids. Just adapt it to the *Post*. They don't want warmed-over Gibson. If they take your stuff, it'll have

to be good. You're a terrible Gibson, but a pretty good Rockwell."[2]

Learn to be yourself. That was part of Ralph's problem, and also Norman Rockwell's. But it's not all there is to being at peace with life.

Chew for Thought

1. Read John 16:33. What does this verse say to you about the nature of true peace?_____

_____

_____

2. How would you describe peace? What is it? Take a look at Philippians 4:6-9 for some more insight._____

_____

_____

FRIDAY

The Ingredient of Love

But, as before, Ralph noticed things weren't right. A good self-image just wasn't enough. Something was still missing. This time he thought for nearly three months before he concluded that what he lacked was love. He'd never really been in love—not like in the movies. Oh, he thought highly of his girlfriend. She was pretty and loving and she knew how to kiss. But she nagged him now and then, and occasionally they had fights. He liked his family a lot. But they were often a bother, especially when he wanted to listen to music in his room. He wanted to feel real love for everyone.

He went to God again.

"You mean you want to learn to be patient, kind, not jealous, and so on?" God asked.

Ralph cocked his head. "In a way," he said. "But I wouldn't want it to become a bother. I mean, I wouldn't want to have to go out of my way all the time."

God appeared dismayed but asked another question. "I guess you don't mean the kind of love that leads a person to give up his whole bank account to help someone in need?"

"Oh, no," said Ralph. "Not that. It's . . . It's the kind of love . . . "

". . . that has a warm feeling in your heart for everyone," said God.

"That's it," said Ralph, looking up. "How did you know?"

God sighed. "You ask a hard thing, Ralph Pyle. But yes, I know the kind of love you want. I've seen much of it. I guess I've always found a way to supply it. So why not you?" he said, shaking his head. "Go your way. I'll try to answer."

The answer was slow in coming. But gradually, Ralph noticed that he began to have nice feelings toward some people. He found he actually liked a lot of people. Not to the point that he really did anything for them. But he began to describe himself as a humanitarian. "I care about the race," he said. "I hope we all get it together."

Sometimes he thought about writing a letter to his congressman about some problem. On one occasion, he even gave a little money to an organization that helped orphans. He felt great after that. He had become a nice guy.

But, of course, it wasn't enough. He still lacked something.

Grazing

Real love can't come in "little bits." It's got to be all out. You can't love quarter way or half way. It requires a total commitment, a total giving. Ralph's quest for meaning in life was strangled by his desire for just enough love to get by. What kind of love are you looking for?

Becky Pippert writes of a young nurse who learned to see the image of God in some of her most helpless patients. "Eileen was one of her first patients, a person who was totally helpless," she writes, quoting a story in a magazine. " 'A cerebral aneurysm (broken blood vessels in the brain) had left her with no conscious control over her body,' the nurse writes. As near as the doctors could tell, Eileen was totally unconscious, unable to feel pain and unaware of anything going on around her."

The jobs of turning her to prevent bedsores and feeding her were so disgusting that many nurses simply tuned out emotionally when they were in her room. Eileen was regarded as a thing, little more than a vegetable. Frequently, nurses made cutting and gross jokes about her and her room.

"But this student nurse," Pippert says, "decided that she could not treat this person like the others had treated her.

She talked to Eileen, sang to her, encouraged her, and even brought her little gifts. One day when things were especially difficult and it would have been easy for the young nurse to take out her frustrations on the patient, she was especially kind. It was Thanksgiving Day and the nurse said to the patient, 'I was in a cruddy mood this morning, Eileen, because it was supposed to be my day off. But now that I'm here, I'm glad. I wouldn't have wanted to miss seeing you on Thanksgiving. Do you know this is Thanksgiving?'

"Just then the telephone rang, and as the nurse turned to answer it, she looked quickly back at the patient. Suddenly, she writes, 'Eileen was looking at me . . . crying. Big damp circles stained her pillow, and she was shaking all over.'

"That was the only human emotion Eileen ever showed any of them, but it was enough to change the whole attitude of the hospital staff toward her. Not long afterward, Eileen died. The young nurse closes her story, saying, 'I keep thinking about her . . . It occurred to me that I owe her an awful lot. Except for Eileen, I might never have known what it's like to give myself to someone who can't give back.' "[3]

That's the kind of love Ralph Pyle needed but didn't know enough to ask for or give.

Chew for Thought

1. For some insight into real love read 1 Corinthians 13:1-13. What do you learn about love from this passage?___
_____
_____

2. Which quality of love in 1 Corinthians 13 do you feel you're weakest in? How can you demonstrate that quality today?_____
_____

WEEKEND

The Real Thing

After nearly a year of thinking about it, one morning it hit Ralph. "I want to go to heaven when I die. But I don't have real faith," he exclaimed. "I lack faith. I'll go to God and talk with him about it immediately."

Before he went, though, he decided to read the Bible. Many hours he meditated on such statements as, "He who does not take his cross and follow after Me is not worthy of Me." And, "Take My yoke upon you, and learn from Me, for I am gentle and humble in heart." He also watched Christians—in church, out of church, in the home, out of the home.

Finally, he formed his petition. "I want to be able to go to heaven when I die—maybe I need some faith."

"Do you want the faith that moves mountains?" asked God, pleased.

"Oh, not all that much," said Ralph, smiling. "I just want enough faith to get me to heaven."

God's face took on a dark look. "Do you not want the faith that takes up its cross and follows my son wherever he goes?"

"Not that much," replied Ralph. "Just enough to keep me out of hell."

God appeared angry, but Ralph kept smiling. He'd done everything else, he thought.

"Do you want the faith that obeys my word, studies my truth, and yearns for righteousness, meekness, abundant life?"

Ralph said, "The abundant life part, yes. But those other things I don't think I really need. I just want enough faith to make me a decent American."

God sighed a long, heavy, dark sigh. He said, "Ralph

Pyle, you ask the impossible. There is no such faith."

Ralph laughed. "That cannot be. I've seen this faith everywhere I go."

God shook his head. "Yes, you have seen that kind of faith. But you have not seen real faith. What you ask is impossible. I can give you no such faith. Go your way."

At first, Ralph was greatly dismayed. But then he said to himself, "God can't be right. All these people can't be wrong. Maybe he just had a bad day."

So Ralph lived his faith. And it was a rather fun faith. He was always asking God for things after that: to relieve a headache; to get a raise at work or a parking space downtown on a crowded Saturday. Sometimes God answered, sometimes he didn't. But when he did, Ralph always was most pleased and even told the church about it. He became one of the church's best members.

But it wasn't enough faith to get him to heaven. It wasn't enough to keep him out of hell. It was just enough to make him think he had it made. And that he had a little bit of everything.

Grazing

In the previous six days we've taken a look at a number of counterfeits the devil offers for real meaning in life: possessions, power, popularity, peace, love, faith. But it's necessary to differentiate. What's real? What cuts ice with God?

One of the best verses on faith is found in Hebrews 11:6: "Without faith it is impossible to please [God], for he who comes to God must believe that He is, and that He is a rewarder of those who seek Him." Earlier in the chapter, the author offered an even clearer picture of what faith is. "Now faith is the assurance of things hoped for, the conviction of things not seen. For by it the men of old gained approval" (Hebrews 11:1-2).

There are many different ways of looking at what

counts in life. Being liked. Having everything you want. Attractiveness. Making a mark. Rising to the top of the heap.

But the Bible focuses on one essential ingredient: faith. How do you stand on that issue? Like Ralph Pyle, is your faith in name only?

Karl Barth is considered one of the great Bible teachers and scholars of the twentieth century. Near the end of his life, he was interviewed upon arriving in the United States for one of his many series of lectures. A reporter asked him what was the greatest thought he'd ever had.

Barth thought a long time, then responded, "Jesus loves me this I know, for the Bible tells me so."

When it all comes down to values, meaning, and what counts in life, most of us begin with things like money, beauty, power, and good feelings. But God begins with the kind of faith that believes in his son, follows him, learns to obey him, and ultimately seeks to worship and serve him forever.

Chew for thought

1. Read Mark 9:14-29, with particular attention to verse 24. What does this passage tell you about faith and what it can do? How would you define faith?_____

_____

_____

2. Take a look at yourself. Do you have real faith? Why or why not? What can you do about building it up?_____

_____

_____

Week 1 Notes

1. Charles Colson, *Born Again* (Old Tappan, N.J.: Fleming H. Revell Co., 1976) p. 17.

2. Norman Rockwell, "Autobiography of Norman Rockwell," *Saturday Evening Post*, April 1979, pp. 66-69.

3. Rebecca Manley Pippert, *Out of the Salt Shaker* (Downers Grove, Ill.: Inter-Varsity Press, 1979), pp. 110-111.

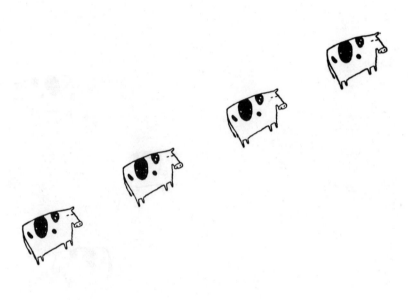

WEEK TWO

Watch Your Step

MONDAY

A New City, a New Style

Dear Beth,

I've cried every day since we left Sacramento. I really miss you and June and everyone. Believe me, Evergreen is no paradise. I feel closed in all the time. I really miss all the kids in the youth group. My dad took us to some church he says is well known all over the country and the pastor's even written some books (big thick ones), but I don't know how much I like it. I went to their Sunday school class. If you ask me, the kids are a bunch of geeks. I know I shouldn't say that, but it's true.

It's not as big a group as we had at Calvary and everyone seems bored. The guy who led the class was kinda rad, but all he did was tell jokes and try to get the class to listen. There were a couple guys who sat over in the corner and mostly looked at the floor, but I caught one looking at me. I found out his name is Jeff. I think he's on the baseball team or something—he had a letter jacket. He's tall, with curly brown hair. He wears it short, but nothing weird (like a buzz or something; I can't believe some guys wear them!). Anyway, I'm dreaming. I want to be back in CA.

I'll be getting my driver's license this summer—if I take Driver's Ed. Wasn't Mr. Summers great? I hope I get another teacher like him. I really miss Fielding High. Wasn't that beach party perfect? If only Bill had gotten up the nerve to ask me out, last year would have been the best. As for here, I'm looking forward to Evergreen's "nationally rated" program (HaHa). Sounds like a breakfast cereal ad.

Oh, tell June good luck with Harry and to keep partying.

I'm still trying to keep up with my quiet time and all that stuff, but it's hard. It was so great when we could meet in the morning and pray together. I'll never forget you forever. Please write me soon. This place is already old. I could do for something wild.

Well, I better go. It's almost midnight. Love ya.

Cheryl

Grazing

New situations—moving, a change in family life, going away, a crisis—always make us much more vulnerable than the usual day-by-day experiences. In one way, we might feel more open to attack because we're hurting a little inside. But in another way, we're also more on our guard.

A verse that might have appealed to Cheryl at that moment in her life could have been one from Isaiah: "When you pass through the waters, I will be with you; And through the rivers, they will not overflow you. When you walk through the fire, you will not be scorched, Nor will the flame burn you" (43:2). It was a word of assurance to the Israelite people when they were going through a powerful time of trial. No matter where we are or what we face, we can know, if Christ dwells within us, that he is there with us, ready to guide, strengthen, lead, and encourage.

Cheryl probably didn't think, at that time, that she was a prime target for temptation. But be aware that Satan knows precisely where and when to strike at your point of vulnerability.

Years ago, there was a pitcher in the American League who pitched well and completed the year with an excellent win-loss record. Asked what the secret of his success was, he pulled out a little black book. In it he had alphabetized the names of every batter he faced. Underneath their names, he wrote what he pitched to them, what pitches they had the most trouble with, and what pitches they hit. Eventually, he learned nearly every man's strengths and weaknesses. Then he said, "I've learned to pitch to the points where I know a batter is weak."

That's the devil. He throws to your weak points and he'll try to throw you that same way. But you can also take stock in the words of Peter: "The Lord knows how to rescue the godly from temptation" (2 Peter 2:9). And he can rescue you and me.

Chew for Thought

1. Are you in a situation that could make you more vulnerable to temptation? If so, explain how. If not, ask God to make you aware of vulnerable times. _____

_____

_____

2. What areas are your weak points? Where is Satan most likely to succeed in your life? Can you think of some scriptures that might help you? _____

_____

_____

Asked Out

July 3

Dear Beth,

Sorry for the silence. But some good news for once. You remember the guy I mentioned in my first letter, Jeff? Well, we have gone out twice. He's on the baseball team— thank heavens, he doesn't talk about it all the time!—plays short-stop, and he's one of the best hitters. He's in a summer league now and I've gone to two games. Then we went out afterwards to a movie—some comedy with Tom Cruise—not too rad (I didn't tell my parents). I was surprised he took me to something like that (it was rated PG-13—anyway, I'm over 13, right?), but it was a little, as my mother says, *risqué*—(is that how you spell it?).

Anyway, he kissed me on our first date. He took me for a walk in the park. The moonlight was perfect—what am I saying? I must sound like some romantic geek. But it was fantastic. I feel so happy with him. He'll be a senior this fall.

I know you're probably thinking I've fallen in love again. But this time it's real.

Oh, what am I saying? I can hear you laughing now. Okay, go ahead, laugh. But I bet if Jimmy Taylor sat next to you in study hall, you couldn't even get through a page of *Christy* or any other book.

Do you think he could be in love with me? I know, it's too early to tell. I can hear you. But this is so wild. I never felt like this.

I can't believe I'm telling you this—you, the super-evangelist, ultra-conservative, convert-everyone woman. But I know you want to hear everything.

I know you'll probably be calling me after you receive this letter, but don't. Everything's okay. Yes, the youth group is definitely dull, but my dad likes the pastor here. He came out to visit. He gave me—us—the usual lectures. He's not at all like Pastor Dave. But who could match him?

Anyway, things are going very fast. Keep writing. Or call. Sing "Blind Man" for me. Love ya,

Cheryl

Grazing

Dating offers some of life's strongest temptations. When we're with someone we like, or love, it's hard to resist giving in to many of our desires. But one of the greatest truths Christians have is that we have a Lord and Master who understands. Hebrews 4:15 says, "We do not have a high priest who cannot sympathize with our weaknesses, but one who has been tempted in all things as we are, yet without sin." Jesus "was tempted in all things," the same kinds of things we face. Therefore, he knows how to help us when we're in great need.

One of the best examples of what Jesus faced in terms of temptation is found in Matthew 4. Jesus had fasted for forty days and nights. Imagine the hunger he felt on that fortieth day. How he must have wanted just a scrap of food!

It was then that Satan came along and sprang his trap. He said, "If You are the Son of God, command that these stones become bread."

Certainly, some of the strongest temptations are those that involve normal desires, in this case the desire for food. But there are other temptations along the same lines that include the desire for sleep, sex, security, and clothing. Any one of these God-given desires can turn into a temptation to evil when we're asked to violate God's laws in order to fulfill them. In Jesus' case, the Father had not told him he could eat yet. That's why Jesus responded with a quote from Deuteronomy, "It is written, 'Man shall not live on bread alone, but on every word that proceeds out of the mouth of God.' "

Jesus knew what it was to starve. He took his desire to the limits—he knows what it is to take any desire to the limit. That's why he can help someone who's battling temptation on the first, fifth, twelfth, or fiftieth day.

Chew for Thought

1. Read Matthew 4:1-11. What was Jesus' prime way of dealing with Satan's temptations?_____

_____

_____

2. What can you apply from this passage to your own struggles?_____

_____

_____

WEDNESDAY

I Have a Question

September 22

Dear Beth,

I'm really sorry I didn't answer your two letters. And when you called, my mom gave me the message. But I just couldn't talk then. That's why I didn't call back. Everybody's acting strange. My mom and dad have had some bad fights—I don't think his new job is going well. But he was always complaining about work. That's why we came here in the first place.

I'm still going out with Jeff. School's started. He's on the football team, but doesn't get to play much. He was hoping to be first string this year, but some junior beat him out of the quarterback position. He's pretty angry about it—but I can calm him down.

I don't know how to ask you this. I've been wondering about it. I figured you're the best one to ask about it. You probably know six verses right off. But what do you think is okay to do with a guy when you're alone? I don't mean going all the way. I'm against that. But Jeff can be pretty pushy. I know I can be firm with him. I know I love him. I think he loves me. He hasn't said so. But he feels strongly that certain things are all right. I know what Jimmy and the youth leaders drilled into us at Calvary, but sometimes I'm not sure.

Don't worry. Everything's all right. I just wanted your opinion. Don't go writing me a ten-pager now. I'll have to get glasses.

I am kind of depressed. I sort of wish we would just pack up and go back to Sacramento. But I'll be up again this Saturday. Evergreen's playing Centerfield. Big rivalry. Of course, Jeff'll probably be all mad because he didn't start. Oh, well.

Please write me right away, Beth. I'm still homesick.

Love ya,

Cheryl

Grazing

Being raised in a church or even being committed to Christ does not guarantee that a person will always know what's right, what's wrong, and what's up to the individual. Many people faced with temptation don't know what the truth is. They give in because they haven't learned what God says on the subject and why.

Two verses from Psalm 119 are helpful. "How can a young man keep his way pure? By keeping it according to Thy word" (verse 9). "Thy word I have treasured in my heart, That I might not sin against Thee" (verse 11). In order to be convinced that sin is sin and should be resisted, we must often learn why God desires that we abstain from a certain activity, or not go in a certain direction. That's why careful study and memorization of his word are so critical to spiritual health. It's like learning how to run a car. No one would hop into a Maserati without learning which pedals do what and how to shift gears. Similarly, we can't approach life with the attitude of "I'll cross that bridge when I come to it." Sometimes bridges pop up and call for decisions that don't offer us time to consult the road map.

If there is anything in life that has helped me to face and overcome temptation, it's knowing and applying God's word to my circumstances. Knowing why you should not sin a certain sin is often as much a part of the battle as actually refusing to engage in it.

Chew for Thought

1. Read Proverbs 5:1-23. Why should sexual sin be avoided?_____

_____

_____

2. From this passage, what can motivate you to keep clear of sexual sin? _____

_____

_____

THURSDAY

Pressure

November 12

Dear Beth,

This letter is going to be really hard. Please go somewhere alone. I'm scared out of my wits. Beth, please don't get mad. I know we were best friends back at Fielding, and I hope you won't get too upset. But Jeff is really putting on the pressure. I had no idea it would be like this. He says he loves me and certain things are right for love and he can't believe I won't do certain things with him.

I mean, what do you do? I don't want to lose him. But sometimes he makes threats and all sorts of things. I know this is very personal, but I don't have anyone to talk to about it. The youth leaders in the church just aren't like at Calvary.

The worst part of it is that so many girls in my high school class have already done it. I mean the whole way. I can't believe the way they talk about it in gym and the bathroom and study hall. I'm almost afraid ever to say anything. What's so bad about virginity, anyway? Good grief, you'd think it was AIDS the way some girls talk.

Beth, Jeff even asked me if I ever thought I might be a lesbian. That hurt. That really hurt. Just because I won't go all the way with him. I don't know what to say or do. He's so fast and pushy. He won't take no about anything. What am I supposed to do—be the last American virgin? That's what he called me, too. He hasn't told me, but I think he's done it before with another girl, maybe two. I can't believe it. It almost makes me sick.

44

But then he says he loves me and he gets so tender and intimate and romantic. I feel like just giving in and saying okay, I might as well get it over with. He says I don't need to worry about getting pregnant or anything. I can get the pill, or anything I want, at a local Planned Parenthood center. The guidance counselors even keep condoms—is that what they call them?—in their desks. And my parents thought Fielding was bad.

You know the worst thing? I want to do it. I mean the feelings just roll over you. Your whole body is tingling and going crazy and feeling so alive and full. Everything about love is so beautiful and delicious, I find myself just wanting to give in. Why did God make us this way if we're supposed to wait till marriage? That could be another ten years. Maybe never. (Kill that thought!)

Beth, I just thought of something—I don't even know if you're still a virgin. Are you? You don't have to tell me, but it might help for me to know. Do you ever wish you could go all the way? It would really help to know.

I just read over this whole letter—it's 2 A.M. here now—and I know when you read it you'll probably start a prayer chain or something. But please tell me what you think. This is really getting to me.

I love you.

Cheryl

Grazing

Sexual pressure—a natural and normal God-given desire—is one of the hardest temptations of all to deal with. It strikes first when we're young, and God says we can satisfy it only in the context of marriage, which doesn't happen for most of us until we're well out of our adolescence. How then do we keep ourselves pure? "By keeping [our ways] according to Thy word," said the psalmist (Psalm 119:9).

I keep coming back to this, but it's the truth of God's word that is the foundation of all obedience.

However, that's not the end of it. We're looking at a letter from one Christian girl to another and we must remember that we also need the help of our fellow Christians to withstand temptation. Their prayers, ideas, wisdom, presence, and love can be a strong weapon against the forces of darkness. Besides writing her friend Beth, Cheryl might have taken other action as well:

- ◆ Find some Christian friends to whom she could open up and talk.
- ◆ Spend time with adults who could offer her godly counsel on her needs.
- ◆ Involve herself in other activities (psychologists call this "sublimation") so that her natural desires might be given other direction.
- ◆ Refuse to date anyone who didn't have convictions similar to hers.

The thing that kills us in temptation is looking it directly in the face and hoping we can stare it down. We can't. I remember a story about a boy who was trying to save his pennies to buy a birthday gift for his grandfather. One evening his mother heard him pray, "Lord, please help me save my money . . . and don't let the ice cream man come down my street." When God told us to pray that we would not be lead into temptation, he was absolutely serious.

Chew for Thought

1. What kind of pressure have you experienced about sex? How does it feel to be the odd person, the one who is still a virgin? If you have had sex, what godly counsel might you offer others on the issue?_____

out. But I guess it doesn't work that way.

You made me laugh when you told me how to say no. I can't picture you doing that. Did you really tell him that if he put his hand there again you'd slug him? Beth, you're such a scream! How did you get up the courage? And you're supposed to be in love with him! What is more amazing is that Larry didn't touch you after that—and he still kept dating you. Maybe there is hope.

Oh, what am I saying? I know if I do this with Jeff, it's the end. It'll never work. He'll just laugh at me and then I'll have to slug him and I won't be able to. Or what if he slugs me back? I guess if he does, that'll show the real truth of the situation anyway.

Well, you did help me. If your dad makes you pay for the phone call, send me half the bill. It was worth every penny.

Love,

Cheryl

Grazing

The scripture Cheryl was referring to was 1 Corinthians 10:13, "No temptation has overtaken you but such as is common to man; and God is faithful, who will not allow you to be tempted beyond what you are able, but with the temptation will provide the way of escape also."

Notice several facts from this verse. First, no temptation is unique. People all through history have faced the same ones and have overcome.

Second, God is always near and faithful. He sets limits on all temptations in accordance with our abilities and strengths. He won't allow Satan to tempt us "beyond what we are able." Ultimately, that means anytime we give in to temptation we have no right to say, "It was too great; I couldn't handle it." That means that Scripture must be false.

Last, God will provide the "way of escape." It may be over. It may be under. It may be through. Or it may be flee. But he will show us the escape hatch.

If we'll only look.

I remember reading *Run Baby Run* by Nicky Cruz, a one-time gang leader turned Christian. After his conversion some of his old habits were still in place. Nicky had been sexually involved in the past, and although he believed it was wrong, he'd found himself sinking deeper and deeper into temptation. He had prayed that God would help him.

He writes about one night when he and his girlfriend were making out in a park under a tree. One thing led to another, and passions were rising as clothes were being unbuttoned. Then Nicky noticed a burning sensation in his groin. He looked down and found he was covered with biting ants. Both of them jumped up and left.

It paints an almost comical picture, doesn't it? But don't miss the point: God had given them a way of escape!

But that reminds me of another truth. Nicky Cruz could never regain his virginity. But he could find forgiveness and new purity in Christ. That sure gives hope not only to those who have not fallen, but to those who have.

Chew for Thought

1. Read 1 Corinthians 10:13. What do you see that this verse is teaching about temptation?_____

_____

_____

2. Think about the last time you were under sexual pressure. What possible way of escape did you have? Did you use it? _____

_____

_____

WEEKEND

An Amazing Thing

January 12

Dear Beth,

A lot has happened. The principal asked me to give a testimony to the teachers. He said he couldn't do it with the whole student body because he'd probably be sued. But he wanted me to tell them my convictions about things, why I believed it, and so on. It's probably because there are supposedly some twenty-four girls in the high school who are pregnant.

I don't know how he found out about my beliefs. I did talk to two girls in gym. They were talking about abortion and I just decided to say something and soon we were into a discussion about everything. One of them told me she lost her virginity when she was fourteen, and she'd been with over five different guys now and she hated it. The other one didn't say much, but when I finally got up the courage to say I believed in virginity, she said she'd never done it and had been so ashamed that she even lied to others about it.

Anyway, the next thing I knew I was in the principal's office. He asked me some questions about my beliefs, then asked if I would talk to all the teachers one day after school at a local church. He said it would be a voluntary thing, and therefore wouldn't be a violation of any laws. He told me he's a Christian too. I was amazed.

I was so scared. I thought I might wet my pants or something. But after I got up, something calmed me down, and I just talked. It seemed like it only lasted a few minutes, but afterwards my dad told me I talked for twenty minutes. I was amazed.

My dad taped what I said and it's on the tape enclosed. Let me know what you think. I know you've spoken in front of all kinds of groups, but tell me your honest feelings.

Beth, I'm so excited. This is the first time I've had a chance to really stand up for being a Christian. I hope I don't get into any trouble, but it has to be the wildest thing that's ever happened to me.

I guess you want to know about Jeff. Well, I finally told him no, I didn't believe in what he was doing, and I said if he insisted, I wouldn't go out with him anymore. (I didn't have to slug him!) He just stopped calling me. I've heard he's dating someone else already. I hope she can stand up to him, though.

I do feel kind of depressed about that. It hurts especially to see him there in the youth group where we're supposed to be Christians and to know he might be doing that stuff. But I don't know what to do about it. Maybe you can give me some more ideas.

Beth, you've been the greatest friend I could ever have. I hope you can come out this summer and see Evergreen for yourself. Or maybe I can come to Sacramento. I love you. I praise God he put you in my life.

Cheryl

Grazing

Statistics report that over 80 percent of teens in eleventh grade or above are sexually active. That makes it all the more difficult for the average Christian to resist.

But it is possible to resist, and possible to use that resistance as a banner to be proud of, not a symbol of scorn. A passage from Paul comes to my mind, 2 Timothy 4:6-8: "For I am already being poured out as a drink offering, and the time of my departure has come. I have fought the good fight, I have finished the course, I have kept the faith; in the future there is laid up for me the crown of righteousness, which the Lord, the righteous Judge, will award to me on that day; and not only to me, but also to all who have loved His appearing."

Notice what Paul looked forward to, the "crown of righteousness." It's a crown that some believe those who have lived righteous, pure lives will receive from the Lord Jesus at his judgment seat.

It's easy to think in the press and scuffle of battle that we should just give in to temptation, sexual or otherwise. "It's only an act," some say. Others say, "It's fun; why does God want to take away all our fun?"

The truth is that God doesn't want to take away our fun; rather, he wants to give us the very things that will make fun truly fun. What are those things? Righteousness and purity. Only those realities—we might call them holiness of life—will give us the joy, love, peace, and hope we long for.

G. K. Chesterton said, "God paints in many colors, but he never paints so gorgeously as when he paints in white."

Chew for Thought

1. For some more insight read Hebrews 2:17-18 and James 1:12-16._____

_____

_____

2. What principle have you learned about temptation this week? What can you apply in your life today?_____

_____

_____

WEEK THREE

A Bar T Brand in a Bar S World

MONDAY

A Hurting Man's Story

Jesus didn't look different from other teachers. Probably I've heard just about all of them. Always talking and arguing about the Sabbath. I always wondered why it was such an issue.

But I had to admit, Jesus was different. He didn't let them corner him, get him defensive about the Sabbath.

Here he was in our synagogue—well, I should say, their synagogue. They didn't really consider me a part of it with my withered arm and all—I was a sinner. Anyway, here he was teaching on the law and obedience and such and I, for one, wanted to hear him. Tucked back in the shadows I'm not that noticeable. I didn't think he'd object to my being there anyway.

He seemed likable enough. I'd even heard he was doing incredible things—miracles. Healings. Elias told me some time ago that he knew of a blind man who had been healed. But beggars are always lying about something. I've told people who plunked a silver or a gold into my cup that I've been an orphan from childhood. Always a good line. If they knew my own brothers dumped me there every morning to beg, they'd be horrified. But it makes people feel good—like their money was more sacred in the eyes of God because they'd given not only to a cripple, but to an orphan.

Sometimes it made me sick. I felt like cursing people. I imagined myself with a big sword—the kind those Roman soldiers have that you see everywhere—and every time some fancy Pharisee comes to plink his little copper "I'm-such-a-good-person- aren't-I-God" coin in my cup, I'd swing the sword and whack him in half, split from hair to crotch. I'd try to picture it. It made me laugh. Probably the only laughs I ever had.

Of course the rumor about Jesus was that he was an honorable man. However, some said he performed his miracles on the select few, his believers. Sometimes his brusque confidence was hard to take. But he was probably just like the rest. He wanted a name and a following, and his words on the scrolls. Have the scribes quote him on Sabbath. I knew the type.

I was pinching my arm while he talked. It always itched when I thought about it.

And then suddenly he was looking at me. I turned my head to look behind me to see what he was staring at. But I was against the wall. I just hunched down more deeply into my robes. Then he motioned for me to rise.

Grazing

Sometimes we hear about the miracles of Jesus so often in church, we forget what an impact they made on the people involved, both the healed people and the critics. For some, rejection and hatred were a daily reality and burden. Typically, a person with a handicap was considered defective. His deformity was an indication of sin—either his own or his parents'.

While we don't openly reject people because of their physical handicaps, rejection still occurs. But it also occurs for reasons ranging from one's intelligence, race, religion, social status, or ability on the playing field. Poor people can reject rich people and vice versa. The "nerds" might reject the "jocks," as well as the other way around. It can go in any direction, because people will find some way of making others to be inferior, ugly, foolish, or incompetent.

But Jesus looked at handicaps of every sort very differently. The "limitation" exists for only one reason: "that the

2. What can Christians do to deal with the pressure we feel about sex? Why do you think God allows us to feel this kind of pressure? What ways do you see that he has provided to relieve it? _____

_____

FRIDAY

Something to Grab Onto

December 6

Dear Beth,

I want to thank you again for calling. It was so good to hear your voice. Being able to talk for so long really helped. I had no idea that you'd been through the same thing with Larry. But believe me, it was encouraging to know that someone still believes in staying "pure" until marriage.

You know, I just wrote that word "pure" and it almost embarrasses me. Why is that? I'm afraid to speak up in class about anything Christian because of all these new laws and problems in schools. I'm afraid to tell others I'm still a virgin because they might laugh at me. And I'm afraid to tell Jeff a final no for fear that he'll break up with me. It's horrible, all this fear all the time. Why does it have to be this way?

I read over that verse you told me about in 1 Corinthians. I even put it on a card to memorize it. I like the idea that God provides a "way of escape" when we're tempted. I never knew that.

Beth, you'll never know how much it encouraged me for you to tell me what a struggle it's been for you. Love is such a beautiful feeling that you just want to let it take you over. But I liked what you said about saving such a thing for that one special person after you've both made a genuine commitment. I never thought of it that way. I also appreciate you saying that there's nothing wrong with looking at marriage and making vows the foundation of a real commitment. I always thought when you're in love, it should all just work

48

works of God might be displayed in" them. How? Not only by healing, change, or a great victory, for that doesn't always come, but by the attitude which can live in joy, peace, and harmony despite the problem. Who displays the glory of God—a young person with everything going for him or her who uses wit and schemes to succeed, or the person with the withered arm (or the stutter, the JC Penney wardrobe, or the clumsiness on the ball field) who thanks God anyway and serves the Lord in every capacity he or she can?

Chew for Thought

1. Read about another person who suffered rejection in John 9:1-41. What did people believe about him?_____

_____

_____

2. Describe what it feels like to be rejected. Do you know someone who was rejected by others? What could you do to help that person?_____

_____

_____

TUESDAY

Please Don't Notice My Arm, Sir

When Jesus motioned, I didn't think he meant me. But he kept looking directly at me. I have to admit, I was scared. I even began to shake.

He said, "Young man, come forward."

There were rumors that he liked to make examples of people, spin stunning stories. He called them parables. But why was he singling me out?

Okay, I talk big, but I don't like to be noticed. It's my hand. People have called me everything because of it. "Sinner." "Rot-arm." "The worm." I'd rather just sit at my place in the market and beg. I tell lies, sure. But not to everyone.

I pushed my hand deeper into my cloak and turned it away from his gaze. But when he said again, "Young man, come and stand here, please," I stood up.

You don't argue with the likes of him.

After a pause, I stumbled over to him. I dug my arm deeper into my cloak as I edged forward. Real slow. I hoped he'd forget about it. But he didn't. As I stood there trembling and staring at his tawny robe, I tried to think what I'd heard about him. When I looked into his eyes, I flinched. Still, it occurred to me that he might help me in some way.

But my cheek began twitching, and I wanted to go back to my corner.

Grazing

Everyone has hang-ups and our bodies are one of our biggest. Awaking in the morning and discovering a new pimple can kill a whole day. Doing your hair and having it turn out wrong can be upsetting. Being the one on the softball team who always stumbles over his size 11 sneakers can crimp up an otherwise balmy afternoon.

What is to be our attitude about such things? To be sure, we can complain, cry, hide, cake on the makeup, or pretend we don't care. People have done those things precisely because they didn't want to be seen in a "natural" state.

But there's another route. First Thessalonians 5:18 puts it this way: "In everything give thanks; for this is God's will for you in Christ Jesus."

That's a big jump for most of us. How can we "give thanks" for a big nose, or inability at sports, or an alcoholic parent? Our feelings get in the way and we find it hard. But notice what Paul really said. He didn't say, "For everything give thanks." Frankly, there are many things we shouldn't give thanks for; but "in" is another matter. "In" suggests you're where you are because someone else put you there. "In" suggests circumstances beyond your control, but not beyond God's. "In" calls for the ability to see beyond the earthly and into the heavenly.

Joni Eareckson Tada testified to the power of this truth in her best-selling book *Joni*. She became a quadriplegic at age seventeen after a diving accident. For the next few years she was in intensive therapy, trying to regain the ability to move her hands and feet. That ability never came. She was bitter, depressed, and angry. God had cheated her out of everything worthwhile in life. Yet, a change came.

She writes: "Now I wept for all those lost months filled with bitterness and sinful attitudes. I prayed for an understanding of His will for my life. What was God's will for my life? To find out, I had to believe that all that had happened to me was an important part of that plan. I read, 'In everything give thanks, for this is the will of God concerning you.' God's will was for me to be thankful in everything? Okay. I blindly trusted that this was truth."[1]

It was then that Joni gave thanks to God in every-thing—the accident, her quadriplegia, all he had done.

And all he would do.

Chew for Thought

1. Giving thanks in everything is tough. What things can you think of about yourself that you don't like? (You don't have to discuss this with anyone.) Can you give thanks for them, each one, now?

2. Try giving thanks every day for something about yourself—both positive and negative. See if a change comes into your outlook.

WEDNESDAY

Down in Front, Center!

Jesus' eyes roved over the crowd. They sat with set jaws. They were upset about something. The anger was almost tangible, like heat. I knew some hated him. But I didn't know why. I didn't even know why I was trembling so, my heart racing.

I bit my lip.

Suddenly, he said, "Is it lawful on the Sabbath to do good or to do harm, to save life or to kill?"

I almost panicked. Some said he had strange powers, even devilish powers. He could kill me. Right here. In front of everyone. I knew I was a sinner. I knew it. Why else this withered arm?

But weren't other men sinners? Why would he single me out?

My heart beat so loudly I almost couldn't hear what he was saying. I thought maybe I should fall to my knees and beg. But I was afraid my arm would fall out of my cloak, and everyone would see it.

I started to breathe deeply. But he just looked at the crowd. I could tell he was getting angry. His cheek kept flexing.

Still, the question seemed to hang in the air. I wanted to run, but I was rooted to the spot.

Then he spoke again, louder this time. He said, "Stretch out your hand."

Grazing

Most of us would shrink from exposing some personal defect for all to see. But God sees every part of our being—

from our bodies to our past, present, and future. And what does he offer us? Acceptance. Without reservation. Without hesitation. Without cancellation. And with only one condition: faith in Christ. You'll find this guarantee in Romans 8:1-2: "There is therefore now no condemnation for those who are in Christ Jesus. For the law of the Spirit of life in Christ Jesus has set you free from the law of sin and of death."

That's a brand of acceptance none of us should do without.

We all long for acceptance, but occasionally when it looks us in the eye, we're a bit afraid. Can it be true? Can it be real? We don't want to give ourselves to something which may turn out to be false. We've been cheated before.

Years ago, I invited a friend to a concert in Philadelphia. I met him and his date at the entrance to the building, and as we were walking in, I overheard him whisper to his date about me, "He's a real @#$%^&."

Those four little words sting—even today. We've never discussed them. I never let on that I heard. But something went out of our friendship. Maybe secret rejection like that is even worse than the up-front kind.

But that's not what God is like. He says, "I commit myself to you. I accept you. I love you. Forever. No one—not even you—can change that."

Chew for Thought

1. Acceptance is something we all crave and need. What more does the Lord say on the subject? Read Jeremiah 31:3. What does this verse say to you about God's acceptance and love for you?_____

_____

_____

2. Try another passage: Hebrews 13:5-6. Does this encourage you? How?_____

_____

_____

THURSDAY

They Wiggled! They Actually Wiggled!

Jesus' words struck me like a lash. My hand?

I didn't move. I pushed my hand deeper into my cloak and I inched around trying to hide it from him. How did he know anyway?

When I looked up, I was about to plead with him to let me go. Leave me alone. I wouldn't come to the synagogue again. The rabbi wouldn't have to say another word to me.

But Jesus' eyes fell on me and his face seemed to flicker a warmth I hadn't noticed before. Maybe he wasn't going to kill me. But why was he humiliating me?

Then he beckoned me to raise my arm. He wanted to see the hand. He wanted me to stretch it out in front of everyone. I was getting angry. Didn't he understand the arm was dead? I couldn't move it if even Jehovah himself commanded it.

I started to protest, but nothing came out. So I shook my head no, when he commanded me with such force that I nearly jumped.

Instantly, my mind blanked and I jerked the useless arm with all my might—right up into the light. A strange prickly feeling jolted through it. It felt strong—for the first time ever.

I began moving my fingers. They wiggled! They actually wiggled!

Grazing

What a moment! It was something he'd remember all his life, and tell to his family and friends over and over. The Lord had done a wondrous work in him—he'd been healed!

But perhaps there was something more. Jesus had shown that he cared enough to select the man for healing even when he hadn't asked. Jesus had reached out. He had given an unmerited gift. He'd changed the man's life forever.

There were many others Jesus could have healed, but he chose this man. There were others he might have given gifts to, but he selected this one. The man with the crippled hand must have felt accepted, perhaps for the first time in his whole life.

Jesus Christ offers us unconditional, total, and eternal acceptance—if we'll only come. One of the great invitation passages of the Bible captures that idea. It's in Matthew 11:28-30: "Come to Me, all who are weary and heavy-laden, and I will give you rest. Take My yoke upon you, and learn from Me, for I am gentle and humble in heart; and you shall find rest for your souls. For My yoke is easy, and My load is light."

Charlie Shedd once wrote the story of a woman who came to him to give a word of testimony. He had announced to his congregation that he'd welcome hearing stories of ideal husbands. This woman told him that all her life people had made fun of her legs because they looked like tree stumps. She showed them to Dr. Shedd, and he mentally agreed.

She rarely dated in high school because of her legs. But in college she met Mark. She felt a special acceptance from him. Nonetheless, she frequently referred to her legs in cutting terms. One day Mark said to her, "Frances, I want you to quit knocking yourself. I love the way you are. The Lord gave you good, sturdy legs. They give me a solid feeling and I like it." Frances wept as he said it.

Later Mark took her home to meet his mother. She was astonished to discover his mother was crippled. Frances looked at Mark at that moment and felt a love for him like no man she'd ever met. She told Dr. Shedd, "Do you know that was thirteen years ago, and now I can honestly laugh about my legs. Can you see why I say he's wonderful? There isn't one thing in the world I wouldn't do for Mark."[2]

Finding acceptance from someone inspires a loyalty and a love that few of us could ever muster without that acceptance.

Chew for Thought

1. How important to you is acceptance from others? What difference do you see between others' acceptance of you and God's acceptance? Which do you see as more important, more personal?_____

_____

_____

2. Take some time to pray, asking God to make real to you his acceptance of you.

FRIDAY

What Did I Do Wrong?

I looked at Jesus. I said, "It feels different." I felt so stupid the moment I said it. I should have said, "It feels great. Incredible. You healed me."

But when you're nervous, you tend to say dumb things. Then Jesus motioned to me to expose the arm.

I wasn't afraid any more. I threw back the cloak. Even I was amazed. The once-shriveled white hand was alive with vitality. I even flexed it and bent down to touch the ground. I would have started whipping the thing around at that point if he told me to. I was getting excited. I just shouted it out. "You healed me—I'm new."

I almost laughed. I wanted to jump around. To turn to the crowd and bellow out, "I'm healed." But they were so quiet, I just turned and looked at them.

It was strange. Their eyes were like hard inflamed slits. Some spit on the ground. A few turned to go. I looked again at my hand and said more quietly, "But it was withered. It was useless. He healed it."

I didn't know what to do. So I turned to Jesus and asked, "What did I do wrong?"

Grazing

Being accepted by Jesus Christ carries with it a strange price tag: you may be rejected by others because of it.

When I first became a Christian, I discovered a strange problem. For the first time in my life, I felt completely clean and forgiven. The guilt was erased. Hangups I'd battled for

69

years seemed suddenly trivial. There was a joy and fullness that overflowed everywhere I went.

But I found I had terrific problems with some of my friends. For the first time, I sensed a cruel and unyielding rejection from them. They couldn't understand why I stopped swearing, using drugs, drinking, and playing poker. Perhaps they felt I had rejected them. But I was eager to be with them, to love them to Christ. I only wanted them to know this same Jesus who had so transformed me.

Nonetheless, many of them wanted nothing to do with Jesus. "It would cramp my style," one friend told me. "He's a bummer," said someone else. And a third remarked, "He takes away all the good things in life."

I didn't know what to say. But I found that I had to begin building new friendships. Some friendships, which had lasted since third grade, simply dried up and ended. It was hard to accept. But it was either that or forsake Christ.

But there is one beautiful truth about acceptance in Christ: once you're changed inside, you can bear nearly anything outside.

That was what the man in the story would soon find; and you can, too.

Chew for Thought

1. You might want to read a little more about what could happen if you find acceptance from Jesus but not from your friends. Look at 2 Timothy 3:12. _____

_____

_____

2. Have you ever been rejected because of faith in Christ? When? By whom? Why do you think they did this to you?_____

_____

_____

WEEKEND

Believe in Me!

Jesus looked me quietly in the eyes and then turned back to the crowd. His lips were tightly pressed together. He said, "You did nothing."

For a moment I stood there, feeling stunned and afraid. If I had done nothing, then. . . . Suddenly I blurted, "What's wrong then? First they hated me for being a cripple. Now they hate me for being healed. It doesn't make sense."

Most of the crowd just walked out. Some of them were plain hot. But Jesus motioned me to follow him. We walked out into the sunshine. He turned to me and asked, "Do you believe in the Messiah?"

At one time I had, but years of bitterness had just about killed off any faith I had. I was ashamed and hung my head for a moment. But he put his arm on my shoulder. "You have had a difficult time. Don't be bitter against God."

I looked into his eyes. I know I was crying a little, but somehow I felt an inner calm. I said, "I haven't been a good man, Lord."

You know what he said to me? "You're forgiven." Just like that. Then he said, "Believe in me."

That was all.

As I watched him walk away, I looked again at my arm. Healed. Perfect.

I flexed it.

But then I thought about his words, "You're forgiven."

Accepted. Forever. Never again to be turned away.

Tears blurred my eyes. I knew then I had received two gifts that day, and the second was the greater.

Grazing

This one-time handicapped man found an earnest and resilient faith in Christ even though he may never have found acceptance from many of his peers. Yet, God has a way of replacing the old with the new. Though he may have had to leave some of the "old friends" behind who had become hostile to his faith, he undoubtedly discovered new ones who believed as he did.

This is part of what Paul meant in 2 Corinthians 5:17 when he said, "Therefore if any man is in Christ, he is a new creature; the old things passed away; behold, new things have come." You're different. You've changed. You're new. Some folks won't like the change. Some will. Some might renew their ties and become the best of friends. Others might leave forever.

Fred Rogers of "Mister Rogers' Neighborhood" wrote in *Guideposts* about an experience he had as a child at a friend's farm. He'd always wanted to climb around the stone walls that surrounded the property. But his parents would never let him.

Finally, one day he stalked into the drawing room to ask. When no one noticed him he said, "I, uh—I wanna climb the stone walls. Can I climb the stone walls?"

All the women chorused back no, saying he'd hurt himself, he couldn't do it. But then his friend, the owner of the farm, said, "Now hold on just a minute. So the boy wants to climb the stone walls? Then let the boy climb the walls. He has to learn to do things for himself." He told his young friend to get out there and climb those walls, then come back and see him when he was done.

Fred had a great time and finally came in two and half hours later. He went to his friend. The big man said, "Fred, you made this day a special day, just by being yourself.

Always remember, there's just one person in this whole world like you—and I like you just the way you are."[3]

Those words stuck with Fred Rogers for a lifetime. They're words of acceptance. You also have the same kind of words, and you can give them to anyone who crosses your path. The only question is, Will you?

Chew for Thought

1. What does Romans 5:6-11 tell us about God's acceptance of us?_____

_____

_____

2. Just as you have felt rejection from others, you have probably made others feel rejected. Whom might you reach out to today to heal some old wound? _____

_____

_____

Week 3 Notes
1. Joni Eareckson, *Joni* (Grand Rapids, Mich.: Zondervan, 1976), p. 142.
2. Charlie Shedd, *Letters to Philip* (New York: Doubleday, 1968), pp. 6-7.
3. Fred Rogers with Kathryn Brinckerhoff, "I Like You Just the Way You Are," *Guideposts*, September 1980, pp. 3-5.

WEEK FOUR

When Cows Go Bad

MONDAY

The Tape Store

Dave and his best friend Hugh walked into the tape store. "They're fantastic," Hugh said. "And I hear they're even Christians."

Hugh had been telling Dave about a new album from a group called U2. "They're British or Irish or something," he'd said. "But this new album really zings."

It wasn't difficult to find the new tape. Apparently it had hit number one on the charts. There were posters all over the store. It was a dark gray-and-black photo with a desert-like background. One of the band members wore a black punched-up hat. Hugh told him they were a big protest group now.

They rifled through the tapes. U2's tape called "The Joshua Tree" was $10.98. Dave was surprised that Hugh could buy it—he didn't think he had that much money.

Dave wandered down the row looking at the colorful tape covers. He saw many that he would have liked to own—but how could anyone afford them?

Suddenly, Hugh was at Dave's side. "Come on, let's get outa here."

"You're not buying the tape?"

Hugh smiled. "Not right now."

Grazing

There are so many tempting things out there in the marketplace: records, tapes, videos, stereos. It's expensive living in this day and age. A lot of people are pressed to come up with the money to live the way our commercials picture it.

I think Jesus understood what it's like to have all that glittery, glamorous stuff staring you in the face. You want it. But in many cases it's out of reach. We can be tempted to resort to wrong means of getting the right things.

All of us know people who have resorted to wrong means of getting what they want. The question for Christians is, do we let them go on doing it?

This is the issue of confrontation. Contrary to Cain's statement to God concerning the whereabouts of Abel, we are our brother's keeper—in one sense we're all responsible to help someone who is making a mistake or committing sin. How we do that, though, is often difficult.

Chew for Thought

1. Do you ever find yourself wanting things that you can't pay for? Is just wanting something wrong? Why or why not? _____

_____

_____

2. Have you ever confronted someone? What do you think confrontation means? Do you feel that Christians should confront each other? Why or why not? _____

_____

_____

TUESDAY

Five Finger Discount

Hugh and Dave headed out into the mall and walked around. It was winter, and both wore heavy jackets. Hugh wore a military green jacket with large pockets. Dave's was a blue ski parka. He skied nearly every weekend with his family in the Pennsylvania mountains.

Hugh put his hand in his pocket and drew out a package. Instantly Dave recognized the U2 tape.

"I thought you weren't going to buy it."

"I didn't."

"You didn't! Then what ... "

"Five-finger discount, man."

Dave gaped a moment at Hugh. He had never known Hugh to be dishonest.

"You can't do that," he sputtered.

"What do you mean I can't? I just did." Hugh grinned. "Saved eleven bucks, plus tax, sonny boy. Think of it as an investment in my future tape collection."

"You mean you've done this before?"

Hugh rolled his eyes and looked away. "Think I'm up to my seventeenth tape this year. Those people in that store have the IQs of rats."

Dave swallowed and glanced around the mall. Suddenly he was afraid they'd be followed, or a policeman would walk up to them and make an arrest. He looked at Hugh again. For so long he and Hugh had been best friends. Why hadn't he known?

Dave tried to think of what he should do. Was he supposed to act like nothing was wrong, or should he have nothing to do with Hugh? Both ways seemed wrong, but what was right?

79

Suddenly, Dave said, "Hugh, I don't like this."

Hugh smiled. "You don't have to. It's my gig. Now let's go listen to the music."

Grazing

Shoplifting in America is at an all-time high. When you go into a store and make a purchase today, some of the money you pay goes toward the costs the store incurs because of theft. Often, people begin shoplifting in their early years. When they find it's easy and the fear lessens, they may try bigger heists.

But for Dave as a Christian, this situation was most disconcerting. What was he to do—just let Hugh continue? Or should he say one thing, then leave it to Hugh to determine what to do? Or should he just duck out, pretending he didn't know or care?

James had a good word for us as a starting point. He said, "My brethren, if any among you strays from the truth, and one turns him back, let him know that he who turns a sinner from the error of his way will save his soul from death, and will cover a multitude of sins" (James 5:19-20).

Clearly, James had no thought of "hoping the problem goes away." He calls us to action. "If you see a brother sinning," he might say, "you have to stop him. You could literally save his soul from death in the here and now, and maybe from condemnation to hell in the hereafter."

In the concluding scene of Shakespeare's play *Romeo and Juliet*, Juliet has been found lying over the body of the poisoned Romeo, a dagger in her breast. The whole story comes out from the Friar, who gave Juliet the potion that would let her sleep until Romeo could rescue her. But all has gone awry, and now both lovers are dead. It's the word of the Prince that somehow brings it all to a close. His speech runs sharp with bitterness and cruel regret. The fathers of the two houses whose rivalry has split Verona stand, heads bowed. Their wives and other kinsmen stand about them, weeping and heavy hearted with guilt.

The Prince speaks to all of them.

"Where be these enemies? Capulet, Montague,
See what a scourge is laid upon your hate,
That heaven finds means to kill your joys with love.
And I, for winking at your discords too,
Have lost a brace of kinsmen. All are punished."

The line that has always struck me is the one that says, "And I for winking on your discords . . . " Here was a man who saw that he'd done nothing when people around him sinned. In the end, "All are punished!"

That's what Dave would be doing, though, if he left Hugh to his own devices—"winking" on his sin. Can any of us stand by and watch someone destroy himself? Especially when we could do something to stop him?

Chew for Thought

1. Read the Ten Commandments in Exodus 20. Why do you think stealing is wrong? Is it always wrong? Can you think of a situation where it might not be, and why?_____

_____

_____

2. Have you ever stolen something? If so, would you be willing to go back and correct what was done by paying for it?_____

_____

_____

WEDNESDAY

Why Do I Have to Know about This?

Dave felt uncomfortable and hot as he listened to U2 with Hugh in his room. The music was all right. But he couldn't listen. He felt guilty.

Meanwhile, Hugh showed him the other tapes. All rock, but a few Christian albums. One by a group called Stryper.

"I figure I've saved some two hundred big ones so far," Hugh said with pride.

Dave swallowed and chewed his lip. He didn't know what to do. He knew this wasn't right. But he couldn't just turn his best friend in to the police. He coughed and said, "I need to use the bathroom."

Hugh motioned him out of the room. "I'll keep the tape player hot."

Dave stood in the bathroom and looked at his face in the mirror. "This is ridiculous," he murmured. "Hugh is vice president of the youth group."

He looked himself up and down. He'd grown a lot in the last year. He was nearly six feet tall, two inches taller than Hugh. Hugh was on the wrestling team. Dave played JV basketball. Still, he felt himself shaking. "What am I so scared about?" he whispered.

Was it that Hugh might hit him or start a fight? That their friendship would end?

That was a real possibility. Maybe that was it . . . Hugh might cut him off—forever.

But wasn't caring enough to stop someone from doing wrong the essence of friendship?

Dave flushed the toilet and looked at himself in the mirror again. He ran his fingers through his dark hair. He felt like cursing. "Why do I have to know about this?" he murmured again as he walked out.

Grazing

Someone once asked me if I wanted to know about some of his pet sins. I thought about it, then I said, "No." He laughed and asked me why. I told him I didn't want to know, because then I'd have to confront him about it and I hated confrontations. I told him, though, that if he knew they were sins, he should stop.

He told me he was only kidding.

Sin is a serious issue. It is so serious that God sent his son to die on the cross so that our sins could be forgiven. Dave now had a decision to make. Should he stand by and watch Hugh continue to steal?

A verse that Dave might have consulted if he wanted to find out what the Bible said about it is Galatians 6:1: "Brethren, even if a man is caught in any trespass, you who are spiritual, restore such a one in a spirit of gentleness; each one looking to yourself, lest you too be tempted."

Dave's motive for confronting needs to be to restore his fallen brother—not to berate him, put him down, or reject him for his sin. Sometimes people gain a lot of pleasure from pointing out another person's sin—it allows them to justify their own behavior.

But, even if your motive is pure, confrontation can provoke hot words. Two friends can cease to be friends. Two neighbors might begin a feud. Whole families could clash. It's not easy.

No one likes to be told he's a sinner. That was Dave's problem. How could he tell his friend Hugh that he was sinning, without resorting to anger or name-calling?

Chew for Thought

1. Jesus knew the importance and the problem of confronting sinners. Take a look at how he handled one in Luke 10:38-42. How would you describe Jesus' style?_____

_____

_____

2. What do you think you would do in this situation with Hugh? How would you handle it? What scriptures would you use as guidance?_____

_____

_____

THURSDAY

Is It None of My Business?

On the way home that night, Dave argued with himself. "It's none of my business," he said. "If Hugh wants to rip off a music store, what's that to me?"

But another voice within him said, "Hugh's supposed to be a Christian. The commandment says, 'You shall not steal.' It's not right."

Dave breathed out heavily and turned into his parents' driveway. He suddenly found himself praying, "What am I supposed to do, Lord? He's my best friend."

That evening he ate little at dinner and went up to his room. He wasn't the kind of Christian who read his Bible a lot. He knew where the books were and so on, but he wasn't sure where to look for help. Suddenly he picked up the phone and dialed his youth pastor's number.

Tom Jarrett was a graduate of a nearby Bible college. He frequently took the group on camping outings to the beach and mountains. He was a rough-and-tumble type of person, and Dave liked him. At times he hoped he would be like him when he reached his twenties.

Tom answered.

"Tom, it's Dave Hogan."

"Hey, Dave! What's up?"

"Just got a question for you. Do you know any scriptures or anything about what to do when a fellow Christian does something wrong?"

"Sure. Are you talking about a situation you know about?"

"Sort of."

"Are you sure it's sin and not just a gray area?"

"Definitely."

"Okay, get your Bible. I'll tell you a few passages and you can look them up and read them on your own."

Tom gave Dave five different passages relating to sinning Christians and confrontation.

Grazing

We've already looked at some of those passages in previous lessons. But here's another, 2 Thessalonians 3:14-15: "If anyone does not obey our instruction in this letter, take special note of that man and do not associate with him, so that he may be put to shame. And yet do not regard him as an enemy, but admonish him as a brother."

That word *admonish* is the key idea. It means not only to confront someone about sin, but to warn and instruct him or her. Correction is the idea. Gentle persuasion from a heart that cares.

Several years ago a friend took me out to lunch. I thought the purpose was purely social. But after we'd eaten, my friend said, "There is a reason I wanted to meet with you today."

She then went on and detailed a number of problems she saw cropping up in my life. Little dishonesties. Giving in to others too easily about things that were wrong. Pretending there was no problem when there was. These were things I was aware of but which I had hoped were hidden from people like her. I was cut inside, convicted deeply. I knew it was sin.

But it was her gentle manner that encouraged me. She took my hand and told me that the only reason she'd confronted me was because she cared. She didn't want to see me hurting myself and my family.

I took what she said, went home, and began working and praying towards change. Sometime later I asked her if she'd seen any improvement. She said, "So much that I'd forgotten about it."

I was grateful and encouraged.

I believe what she had done with me was biblical admonishment. It was gentle, kind, loving. Not a curse-laden cry in the middle of an argument. Or a bottle of Scope in my mailbox. It was direct, straightforward confrontation that minced no words but also expressed love.

Confrontation doesn't have to be loud or mean. It can be one of the most exhilarating and freeing experiences in life—for those who desire to change.

Chew for Thought

1. You can read about how the Lord confronted different people in other passages: Genesis 3:8-24 and 4:1-15. Describe God in these sections. How does he feel about sin?_____

_____

_____

2. What gives you the greatest fear about confronting someone about sin? Be specific. Why do you think it's troublesome to you?_____

_____

_____

FRIDAY

Matthew 18

The passage that related most directly to Dave's problem was something Jesus said in Matthew 18:15: "If your brother sins, go and reprove him in private; if he listens to you, you have won your brother." But he especially liked the real life situation Tom told him about in 2 Samuel 12 where Nathan confronted David about his sin with Bathsheba.

Dave was sure he needed to do something with Hugh. He couldn't let him continue to steal. But how could he talk to Hugh more directly about it without Hugh blowing up or even rejecting him as a friend? Hugh had long demonstrated a fierce temper, and he and Dave had fought more than once. Hugh always won. Though they hadn't had a bitter dispute in several years, Dave had vowed never to get into something like their last fight during a back-lot football game. Hugh belted him in the nose, and though Dave tackled him and knocked him to the ground, it had taken them both several weeks to face one another.

Dave meditated on the passages he'd read. Finally he prayed and asked for God's guidance. But he knew very well, God wasn't going to make it all disappear. He thought about talking to Tom again before he did anything, but he decided to take Jesus' words in Matthew 18:15 literally: "reprove him in private." He didn't feel he should let anyone know about what was going on, unless it went to that second step.

He tried not to think about what that meant.

That afternoon after basketball practice, he headed over to Hugh's house. His mother said he was in his room. Before entering, Dave made sure once again he had his little pocket Bible in his jacket pocket.

"Hey, what's up?" Hugh said and jumped off his bed. The music was loud. Dave didn't recognize the band.

"Something new?" Dave said.

Hugh winked and said, "Yeah, I got it yesterday afternoon, if you know what I mean."

Grazing

If there is a key passage on confrontation in the Bible, it's Jesus' statement in Matthew 18:15-17: "And if your brother sins, go and reprove him in private; if he listens to you, you have won your brother. But if he does not listen to you, take one or two more with you, so that by the mouth of two or three witnesses every fact may be confirmed. And if he refuses to listen to them, tell it to the church; and if he refuses to listen even to the church, let him be to you as a Gentile and a tax-gatherer."

Notice several important thoughts from the passage.

- This applies to a fellow believer. It's not something you do with just anyone.
- Be sure what he or she is doing is sin, not just a matter of differing opinion or a "gray" area of Christian living.
- Don't wait for him or her to do something or invite a confrontation. Take the initiative.
- Point out the sin. Just having someone else know that you're sinning is often enough to stop you.
- Do it "in private." No one else should know about it. It's critical, both for your feelings and the other person's.

If you can't tell a friend something you think is wrong, what kind of friendship do you have? Ben Franklin said, "'Tis great confidence in a friend to tell him your faults, greater to tell him his."

Friday

Chew for Thought

1. Another example of confrontation occurs in Joshua 7:1-26. It's a very tense and difficult situation. How would you have handled it if you were Joshua?_____

_____

_____

2. Why do you think confronting others, even Christians, gives us so much fear? What can be done about it biblically?_____

_____

_____

WEEKEND

Thanks, Brother

Dave sat down on the edge of Hugh's bed. He asked Hugh to turn the music off. Hugh gave him a quizzical look, then turned off the stereo. He sat down on the bed.

"All right, what's all the mystery about?"

Dave cleared his throat. His mouth was dry. His heart pounded. He felt like forgetting the whole thing. But he pressed on. "Hugh, this stealing isn't right."

Hugh snickered. "Come on. Is this what you're upset about?"

Dave fixed his eyes on Hugh. "I'm more than upset, Hugh. It's wrong. You know it. I know it. And if anyone else saw you do it, they'd say so too, especially someone from the church."

"Oh, come on, everyone does it." He paused. "Except maybe you."

Dave tightened his lips. He fought hard to talk evenly, but his words came in little gasps. "Hugh, this is before God. And Jesus. Do you think this pleases him?"

Suddenly, Hugh was on his feet. "Look, Holy Joe, who do you think you are? I've done more for you than anyone on earth . . ."

Dave was on his feet. "It's not a matter of all you've done for me," he snapped. Then he caught himself. He closed his eyes and stopped; he sat down. He sighed and went on. "Hugh, it's just that I don't want to see you do something wrong. I care about what you do with your life. I don't want to see you go the wrong way."

For a moment, Hugh stood there appearing to waver between wanting to give Dave a smack and wanting to run.

91

He sat down and bowed his head.

"Yeah," he muttered. "I know you're right." He looked up. His face twitched. "Have you told anyone about this?"

Dave explained about calling Tom but assured Hugh he hadn't said anything about what was going on.

Hugh shook his head. "I knew I shouldn't have done it. But . . . " He sighed. "I don't know."

Dave breathed out heavily, then said, "Hugh, you have to return the tapes."

Hugh nodded. "I know."

Dave put his hand on Hugh's shoulder. "I'll go with you. Let's get it over with. Okay?"

Hugh looked up. Suddenly, they both embraced. "Thanks, brother," he said.

Grazing

Not all confrontations have a happy ending. But in most cases, you never get to the second step of Jesus' process, or the third. Most Christians turn around after a first talking-to.

When I was in college my father confronted me about a problem I had with manners. Being in a college fraternity had unfortunately done a job on my table talk and social graces.

One night we sat down to dinner. When Dad sat down, he didn't say grace or even say hello. He dug right in with a loud grunt.

I watched, fascinated. To me, it was hilarious.

Then he wanted the salt. He didn't say, "Pass it," he simply reached across my chest and grabbed it.

I started laughing—I couldn't believe his rudeness.

Then Dad said, "Guess who I'm being like?"

I had no idea, but whoever it was, it sure was funny! "You!"

I was stunned, then convicted. My father got his point

across, and I began the great reformation. He was very gentle with me after that.

If confrontation means anything, it means being loyal and loving enough to stick with and work with someone even though you may feel that person's done something wrong. Being loyal means not gossiping about it to someone else, not running the person down, but going personally and in private, and sharing your concern.

Most of all, it means not committing the sin yourself.

Chew for Thought

1. Take a final look at how Jesus confronted someone in John 4:1-26. How do you feel about how Jesus handled this situation? How would you have handled it?_____

_____

_____

2. Is there someone you may need to confront? Who? Why? What scriptures would you use to back up your convictions?_____

_____

_____

WEEK FIVE

When they're in Too Deep

MONDAY

A Chance Meeting

Jill stalked down the hall towards the girls' bathroom. *What you had to do to get Miss Johnson to allow you to get a pass! Honestly,* she thought, *you'd think the lady never had to go herself!*

She pushed open the door and looked in. Empty. She headed for a stall. The first one was closed. She walked into the second one. Suddenly, two quick sniffles cut the silence from the stall next to hers. Someone was there.

Jill waited. There were more sniffles, then a muffled crying.

She wondered what to do. Should she just ignore it and leave? Or . . .

She started to say something, then stopped. *What if she doesn't want help?* she thought.

She concentrated, but the muffled sobbing made it hard to think. No, she should offer to help even if the girl didn't want it. She took a deep breath.

"Are you all right?" she asked. She could feel her heart jumping in her chest.

No answer. More sniffles. More muffled crying.
She took another breath. "Can I help?"
There was a choked reply. "No one can help."
Jill went out of the stall and stood in the aisle. She hesitated, then knocked on the door. "Can I do anything? Are you all right?"

There was a long sigh. "I don't know," the voice said.
Jill stammered, "I just want to help. I won't tell anyone."
"Sure."

That caught her off guard. What should she say now?
She hesitated again. But now she felt more committed.

She wanted to help. "Look, if you just want to talk, we'll talk. You don't even have to open the door."

There was a long, uneasy silence.

Then, "It's my parents—they're getting a divorce. My mom told me this morning."

Jill waited. *A divorce!* She thought about what that must feel like. Then, should she say anything more? No, just listen, she told herself.

"They had a huge fight last night. They're always fighting."

After a long pause the latch turned, and the door came open slowly. It was Eva Martin. Her eyes were red and her makeup smeared.

Jill prayed for wisdom. "I really want to help, Eva. Would you like to talk more?"

Grazing

It's obviously not a simple situation to solve. Here's a person suffering from a circumstance she has no control over. What would you do? What would you say?

What problems have you known people to carry over the years? Have you ever known someone . . .

whose mom or dad was dying?

who studies hard but doesn't do well in school?

whose father is out of work and the family doesn't have
    enough money to live?

who was fired so that the boss's son could have a job?

who is always the butt of everyone's jokes?

who is trying to adjust to living in a blended family?

who always sits alone at lunch?

Do you know anyone who is troubled? How could you help? What would you do to help Eva?

Chew for Thought

1. Read about Ruth and Naomi in Ruth 1. What do you see that Ruth did to help her stricken mother-in-law?_____

_____

_____

2. Think of someone you know who is hurting. How might you reach out to that person? Name one practical step. To get an idea, read Matthew 5:1-9. _____

_____

_____

TUESDAY

No One Can Help!

Jill listened as Eva poured out the story of a mean-spirited father who argued constantly with her mother. It was so bad Eva was ashamed to invite people over. Several times she'd made excuses when friends wanted to come in after they'd dropped her off at her house after a game. It made some of her friends angry—but she was too embarrassed to tell them the truth. Now everyone would know.

"Look," Jill said, after listening to Eva's story, "I'd like you to talk to a friend of mine. He might be able to help. He's helped me before."

"Who is he?" Eva's eyes flickered with the slightest glimmer of hope.

"He's one of our pastors at church."

"No way!" said Eva. "I've done that before. Then they're telling your whole story to everyone."

"He won't tell," Jill said flatly. "I know. I've told him some things. He doesn't tell people about other people's problems."

Eva bit her lip and looked away. "He's not going to preach at me is he?"

Jill shook her head. "He's really a good guy. Maybe . . . Look, I'll call him. We can meet you in back of the cafeteria after school. School'll be out in—" she looked at her watch "—in another half-hour."

Eva looked down and sighed. "I don't know. I just don't know what to do."

Jill looked at her. Eva seemed calmer now. But there was a lump in Jill's throat. She thought of her own parents. What would it be like to have a dad and mom who couldn't get along?

"I promise," she said, "we won't force you into anything. Just talk. That's all. I promise."

Eva looked up. There were tears in her eyes. Then she looked down and nodded her head. "Okay. I have to talk to someone who can help."

Jill breathed out deeply. "Good. Look, you shouldn't have to sit in here. Let's go down to the student lounge. You can . . ."

"No! I don't want anyone to see me."

Jill swallowed. She felt a mixture of fear, anger, and hope all at once. She only prayed that Ken would be able to come. "All right. But you'll meet me after school?"

Eva nodded.

Jill turned and went out of the bathroom to the phone booth to call her youth pastor.

Grazing

Divorce is at an all-time high. How a teenager faces living in a broken home defies easy solutions. There's no magic answer to the problem. Eva needs people who care, who love, who can help her through this difficult time.

Jesus told a potent story about helping others in Luke 10:25-37. We call it "The Story of the Good Samaritan." There are not many of them around nowadays. Looking at the story, notice a few things about it. First, several people had an opportunity to help, but only one did. Similarly, each of us has to be aware of the incidents God brings our way. If God is sovereign, and he is, then he allows disasters and problems to happen for a purpose.

Second, the beaten man's problem was an inconvenience for the Samaritan. Certainly he was on his way somewhere, and he wanted to get there quickly. But the other man's need took precedence. In the same way, take a look at the things that you regard as "inconveniences." Could they be there because God wants to bless both you and the other person regardless of any inconvenience for either?

Third, there's no mention of the Samaritan ever getting any recognition or repayment for his deeds. But he had a reward. From where? From God himself. One day the Lord would reward him for his goodness.

Ever feel like you're rushing through this world with little care for anyone but yourself? God wants us to shed that outlook. He desires that we take a look around, spot a need, and meet it. That's the essence of caring for one another.

Chew for Thought

1. Read the story of the good Samaritan in Luke 10:25-37. Can you think of any opportunities God has given you or is giving you that might be a chance to be a neighbor to someone else? _____

_____

_____

2. Give some examples of how others have helped you. How did you feel about them, about what they did? _____

_____

_____

There Must Be Some Way to Help

Jill's youth pastor, Ken Stoner, met her after school behind the cafeteria. Eva wasn't there. They waited for thirty minutes.

"I really thought she would come," Jill said.

"Maybe she's just not ready," Ken answered. "Maybe she needs a little time. But why don't we think of some things we can do to help her?"

Jill and Ken talked for a few minutes, then Jill pulled out a piece of paper and listed several ways she could help Eva.

Pray.

Go out of my way to talk to her each day. Build a friend-
    ship.

Listen.

Invite her again to a youth group meeting.

Invite her over to my house for a meal or a weekend.

Take her on a retreat.

Encourage her to talk to a counselor.

Pray with her.

When she looked back over her list, she looked up at Ken. "Some of these are pretty hard," she said. "I mean, if I do them it'll take time and maybe even money."

Ken smiled.

Grazing

One of my favorite quotes is this: "Be kind. Everyone you meet is fighting a hard battle."

I'm certain Eva was fighting one of the hardest battles of her life. But so was Jill. This was new to her. She didn't have a life like Eva's. What would you do if you were confronted with a situation like this? What scriptures might you share with someone like Eva? Strangely enough, Psalm 23 might be a good starting place. You probably know the words, but let's look at them:

> "The LORD is my shepherd,
> I shall not want.
> He makes me lie down in green pastures;
> He leads me beside quiet waters.
> He restores my soul;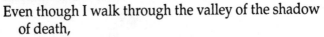
> He guides me in the paths of righteousness
> For His name's sake.
> Even though I walk through the valley of the shadow
>   of death,
> I fear no evil; for Thou art with me;
> Thy rod and Thy staff, they comfort me.
> Thou dost prepare a table before me in the
>   presence of my enemies;
> Thou hast anointed my head with oil;
> My cup overflows.
> Surely goodness and lovingkindness will follow me
>   all the days of my life,
> And I will dwell in the house of the LORD forever."

God is with us in every circumstance of our life.

Chew for Thought

1. Repeat Psalm 23 several times and imagine the scene of the shepherd and his sheep. Then take a moment and put yourself into the psalm. The words have a power all their own.

2. What can you do to build a bridge today with someone? Name the person and write down what you can do, then try it._____

_____

_____

THURSDAY

It Takes Work and Effort

Jill reached out to Eva. For several weeks it was as though Eva didn't remember their talk in the bathroom. Then one day Jill ran into her outside the gym. She was leaning up against the wall, alone. Jill walked over to her immediately.

"Eva, hi!"

Eva smiled weakly.

"I've missed you. I hope things are better."

Eva looked at the ground and dug her toe into the dirt. "I guess so—my dad's moved out."

Jill waited. She didn't believe things were OK, but she wasn't sure what to say. But something occurred to her, and she said, "Look, we're all working on this English project now about John Donne. Would you like to study together one afternoon?"

Eva cleared her throat and looked away. "Not really."

"I don't know," Jill went on. "I found some good stuff in a reference book. Maybe we could go out for cokes afterward."

Eva suddenly looked deeply into Jill's eyes, then flinched away.

Jill waited. She sensed that Eva was making a hard decision. She had never realized how difficult it is for some people to reach out, or to let others reach out to them. Somehow she knew she'd have to be patient and go at Eva's pace, not hers. She tried to pray, to think, but she only hoped Eva would open up.

Then Eva said, "Okay," barely audibly.

Jill smiled. She was about to say something about studying that afternoon, then she thought maybe that would be pushing it. Still, something inside her seemed to signal a go-ahead, if she could be easy about it. "Well, I'm going over to the library this afternoon. Would you like to make it today?" She tried to make it sound casual, like it was all right if Eva didn't want to.

"All right. I'll meet you in the library."

Jill swallowed, then glanced at her watch. "Well, better get to class. Would you like to walk together?"

Eva nodded and Jill turned to go.

Grazing

Frequently, people do not respond immediately to our care. We have to make an effort, give it time, work at it. Even God treats us that way. He never expects us to change or grow immediately. He often works with us for many years before we see steady and powerful growth in our lives.

One of my favorite scriptures is found in Philippians 1:6: "For I am confident of this very thing, that He who began a good work in you will perfect it until the day of Christ Jesus." God, who began something in us, will complete it.

When we decide to help others, we have to decide we'll complete what we start or at least give all we can. That's not easy, but it's essential in truly learning to serve others.

Sometimes I have wondered if the time we pour into others' lives is worth the effort. Some years ago, I befriended a young man named Alan Saloh. He liked sports and he frequently came by my house to talk and play basketball. He was considerably different from me, struggling with what it meant to be a Christian, what it meant to walk with Jesus.

I tried to give him what I could of what I knew of Christ's love and goodness.

Then I left that city and that ministry, and lost contact with Alan. However, I recently received a letter from one of the leaders of that church who had read an article I'd written.

In her letter were these words: "And remember Alan Saloh? Well, he's gone on with the Lord, participates in church, leads some of the youth now himself, and he's going to be married to a lovely Christian girl he met in the church. It's so wonderful to work with these kids, watch them grow up, and then become fruitful and godly Christians. He often mentions you."

That makes it all worth it.

Chew for Thought

1. Have you struggled with what it means to love someone for Christ's sake? What do you think is required? How do you feel about working with someone for months before you see any benefit?_____

_____

_____

2. Think of someone who has tried to help you over a period of time. Do you ever think that person might have wanted to give up? Why or why not? _____

_____

_____

FRIDAY

No Man Is an Island

As Jill and Eva walked, Jill felt relieved. Maybe Eva would open up. They talked about the basketball game coming up the following night. Jill thought perhaps she'd mention going together, but she'd wait until after the library session. When they reached class, Eva sat at the desk next to hers.

After English, Jill had two other classes and wondered if Eva would really show up. She waited at the library door for several minutes, then went in. A few minutes later, Eva walked in.

Jill showed Eva the reference book she'd found, and they read the passages together. They read Donne's famous words about no man being an island: "No man is an island, entire of itself; every man is a piece of the continent, a part of the main."

After awhile, Jill felt a little playful and read it in a deep masculine voice. The librarian immediately shushed them. But both girls laughed. For the first time, Jill saw Eva smile genuinely.

Afterwards, they had cokes at the local McDonald's. Jill told Eva about her family and several funny stories about her dog, Ripple. But when Eva's eyes welled with tears, she stopped.

"I didn't mean . . ."

"No." Eva waved her hand. "It's all right. I just wish my life was like that." She told Jill more about her own home situation—how the fighting had started after her dad had been laid off from his job several years before.

Jill felt a lump forming in her throat. "I'm sorry, Eva—I wish you didn't have to go through this. I am your friend . . . I want to help."

She wished she could do something more. But what?

As they were leaving, she said, "Oh, Eva, about the basketball game tomorrow night? Some kids from my youth group are going. Would you like to come with us? My older brother has a car and he'll drive us anytime. We can even pick you up."

Eva smiled. "Sure. I'd like that." She smiled again, faintly.

Grazing

Jill's efforts were paying off. I'm reminded of 2 Thessalonians 3:13: "But as for you, brethren, do not grow weary of doing good." "Do not grow weary" pictures a person in a race who is slowing down and then stopping, falling to the ground, and going to sleep. He's grown weary. The work has been too much.

But "doing good" is not for people who get weary. It's work and it often doesn't pay much in this world. But it pays.

Ann Kiemel tells a powerful story in her little book *I'm Out to Change My World*. She grew up in Hawaii. On her campus, she and her sister were the only light faces in the middle of thousands of dark faces. She cried herself to sleep every night during junior high. All the kids she grew up with were Hindus and Buddhists. Kids laughed behind her back because she was a foreigner. They laughed at her belief in Jesus. She didn't fit.

When she'd cry, though, she often asked her daddy, "Why does it pay to serve Jesus?" He answered, "Hang in there. It pays."

When she didn't want to go to school, her mother pushed her out the door, telling her that life is made up of ordinary days. There's no one to pat you on the back. No one to tell you how wonderful you are. But it's how you live your ordinary days that determines whether you ever have a big moment. Her mother would say, "Go out there and make something of your ordinary days."

Ann still remembers that last day in high school. Graduation. She and her sister were on the platform to receive little awards for their grades. As the principal made the announcements, each student would receive slight applause and then he'd go on to the next.

But then the principal called up Ann and her sister Jan. He said, "We're Hindus and Buddhists, but these two girls came and brought God to our campus. They've changed our world."

All Ann can remember was how the applause never seemed to end.

Inside she whispered to herself, "Daddy, you were right. Through the thousands of ordinary days when I wanted to give up, it paid. It pays to follow Jesus."

Chew for Thought

1. Do you feel your days are too humdrum, too ordinary? What can you do to help yourself "hang in there" during the ordinary days we all face?_____

_____

_____

2. Think about the last time you tried to help someone. Did you grow weary? Why? What can you tell yourself the next time you are in a similar situation and want to give up?

_____

_____

_____

WEEKEND

Patient and Determined Effort

Through Jill's patient and determined efforts, Eva began to open up. She and Eva slowly built a friendship. After the basketball game, on another weekday evening Eva came to Jill's house for dinner. Then it was for a weekend where they visited museums and went to a movie in town. Then one Sunday Eva came to church.

From there, Eva began coming regularly. Finally, a year after that first encounter in the bathroom, Eva's parents came for counseling. They hadn't gotten divorced although they were still living apart. It was to be a long battle out of the darkness for them. But it wasn't a battle without hope.

One afternoon nearly two years later, when Eva and Jill were seniors, Eva rushed up to Jill in the hall outside her locker. "Guess what?" she said. "I did it."

"Did what?"

"I accepted him."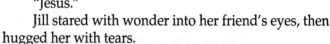

"Who?"

"Jesus."

Jill stared with wonder into her friend's eyes, then hugged her with tears.

"How did it happen? Tell me all about it."

They went to a quieter part of the hall.

"There's not much to tell," said Eva. "I just stopped last night by my bed, knelt down, and asked him to take over. And he did. I know it."

"But why? What led up to it?"

Eva fixed her eyes on Jill's. She said, "You really don't know, do you?"

Jill shook her head.

"Well, it's simple," said Eva. "Because of you. How you've been my friend."

Grazing

Two years! Think of it. The commitment of time and effort and love on Jill's part. But was it worth it? If you asked Jill I think she'd probably say she'd done very little.

But too often we view sharing Christ and loving one another as a "quickie" fix, something that has to see success in thirty minutes or we give up. But that's not reality. There are no fast answers, no immediate changes. It's often a slow go all the way.

Jesus spent thirty years of his life in a carpenter's shop. Then he gave the next three years to twelve men. Three years! How many of us are willing to do the same?

I once read about a soldier who was cut down in action. He cried out to his comrades to drag him off the battlefield and bandage his wounds. But the captain told his men to sit tight. He didn't want to lose anyone else. Nonetheless, the wounded man's friend, a sergeant, jumped out of his foxhole and sped to help his fallen comrade. He began dragging him to safety. In the process he was wounded, and by the time he reached the others, his friend was dead.

The captain shouted at the wounded sergeant. "Why did you disobey orders? It wasn't worth it. Now I've lost two men."

The sergeant gasped, "No, captain, it was worth it. You see, when I reached him, he said to me, 'Sarge, I knew you'd come.'"

There are so many ways to help others with problems—listening, talking, inviting them over to spend the night, spending time together. Perhaps you can think of someone you might do that with today.

Chew for Thought

1. Read Romans 12:9-21. There are many potent directives here about loving others. Which ones speak to you?____

_____

_____

2. Take one of those commands and think of a situation you can apply it to. What one? When?_____

_____

_____

WEEK SIX

That Grass'll Kill You

MONDAY

We Tried It

Josh Evans and his two best friends, Cam Lyle and Jim Galan, sat in the local pancake house. They hadn't seen as much of each other as they'd wanted that summer. They were coming up to their senior year in high school. But with Cam working nights, Jim away as a lifeguard at a summer camp, and Josh playing ball, they simply hadn't gotten together.

The waitress was slow and Jim kept watching the foyer as if waiting for someone. Several times he glanced secretively at Cam. Suddenly, Josh sensed that something was up. He decided to wait, not ask any leading questions. You never knew what Cam had gotten Jim into. But he figured they'd come across at their own speed.

Cam suddenly said quietly, "Well, guess what, Josh?"

Josh shrugged. "I figured you two had something cooking with the way you were acting. What?" But he felt curious, and excited by the tone the meeting had taken.

"We tried it." Cam glanced at Jim again, and Jim rolled his eyes.

"You tried what?" Josh asked. He couldn't think of anything they'd be referring to. There wasn't much left in life that he figured the three of them hadn't gotten into. Except maybe illegal things. But Josh was a Christian, and Cam claimed to be one. And even though Jim wasn't, Josh was sure neither of them would be into something against the law.

Cam looked around at the other diners, then whispered, "Marijuana, Josh. Grass. You know, pot. We got high."

Josh stared at Cam, then at Jim. Suddenly, he sensed

that his mouth was dry and his forehead was sweating. He creaked, "You got high?"

Cam smiled. "It's incredible. We've each done it about five times now. We want you to try it."

Josh looked away and closed his eyes. He felt afraid and angry. They couldn't be into that stuff.

He opened his eyes and stared at Cam and then Jim. "Forget it. I don't do that kind of thing."

Cam snorted. "Don't be a jerk. It's harmless. Anyway, we have some now. We thought we could smoke up a little behind the restaurant."

Josh nearly jumped. "You have some here, right here?"

Grazing

Peer pressure comes in many forms. It runs the gamut from the subtlety of the girl who talks about the designer clothing she has to wear to the hard-line demands and threats the mafia might use to force someone in the group to get involved in extortion. Wherever the pressure you feel falls, it's a real pressure. It can become psychologically overpowering so that you succumb to it like a starved dog. However it strikes you, though, it can lead in many directions—closer to or away from God.

But then there is the pressure some exert to get us to sin, to practice vices we know are evil and should be avoided. Jesus was acutely aware of that pressure. He knew about the many ways it might occur and even warned us about it. In one passage he said, "Watch out and beware of the leaven of the Pharisees and Sadducees" (Matthew 16:6). Watch out for peer pressure.

Everyone's selling something. Most people try to influence those around them to conform to what they consider important. But Christians are to be on the lookout. Whether it's drugs, alcohol, pornography, sex, cutting school, or a multitude of other variations on the theme of sin, it's easy to get pulled in if you're not careful.

In the scene above, Josh's antennae were fine-tuned to what was going on. He knew immediately what he believed about marijuana and drugs. He probably also knew this would not be the end of it. When I was in high school, marijuana was just beginning to invade the average suburban high school. One of my best friends became a "marijuana evangelist," and used every bit of his persuasive abilities to get me to try it. He worked on me for over six months. I asked many questions, fought against the idea, and resisted. But at the time I was not a Christian. I had no scriptural moorings. Ultimately, I gave in and tried it. Through the next five years of my life, drugs were available to me and sometimes I used them.

I felt tremendous pressure. If you're facing it now, believe me, I understand. But I know it's also possible to resist. After I became a Christian, the same pressures were there. Some of my friends rejected me because of my new-found convictions. But it was easier to withstand the pressure because now I not only had new convictions, new Christian friends, and a new heart, but also a Lord who could help me stand. You will find strength in the same resources if you look there.

Chew for Thought

1. Read more from the Bible about how people felt in the face of awesome pressure: David—Psalm 3; Peter—Matthew 26:69-75. What do you think they felt in the midst of their pressurized situations?_____

_____

_____

2. This story is about peer pressure to take drugs. What

type of peer pressure are you under?_____
_____
_____

TUESDAY

Are You Turning Tail?

Cam patted the right pocket on his jeans. "Hey, don't sweat it, man. No one knows." He let his voice fall a little lower. "I bet I could lay it on the table and most people here wouldn't even know what it was. They're not watching."

Josh's heart was racing now. He looked around furtively. There were no policemen in the restaurant, but he knew it was a frequent hangout for some of the locals. He began to push his chair away. "I'm outa here, man. I don't go for this."

Jim coughed and put his hand on Josh's shoulder, holding him in place. "Calm down, dude. You don't want to draw attention to yourself, do you?"

Cam snickered. "I never thought you'd turn tail at something like this."

Josh sat forward and seethed in a whisper, "Look, I don't go messing around with my mind. I don't want to end up in some loony bin. And, if you were smart, you'd wake up and quit this stuff."

Cam set his jaw. "I didn't know you were going to be a jerk about it." He paused.

Josh didn't respond.

"Fine," Cam said. "We'll keep all the fun to ourselves."

The waitress walked over to their table with three plates piled high with pancakes. Jim ate in silence. Josh wondered if he should pray as he usually did before a meal. He decided to offer a silent prayer. *No need to stir them up more than they are*, he thought.

121

Grazing

The pressure is mounting. Notice some of the methods already being used:

> name-calling,
> scorn and mockery,
> telling Josh he's missing something good,
> the silent treatment.

They're all subtle forms of the age-old practice of **peer pressure**. Go through any day with your friends and see how many times such techniques are used without forethought on the part of the user. It comes out in the daily tug and pull of life. We're all born persuaders and pressurizers.

A good passage to bolster your defenses against peer pressure is 1 John 2:15-17: "Do not love the world, nor the things in the world. If anyone loves the world, the love of the Father is not in him. For all that is in the world, the lust of the flesh and the lust of the eyes and the boastful pride of life, is not from the Father, but is from the world. And the world is passing away, and also its lusts; but the one who does the will of God abides forever."

Chew for Thought

1. Think about those verses on "the world" for a moment. What is "the world"? How would you define it? What things would you consider "worldly"? _____

_____

_____

2. Take a look at your own life. In what ways have you been influenced by "the world"? _____

_____

_____

I Said I'm Not Interested

After finishing breakfast, the three walked out in silence. Cam and Jim headed toward their car, but Josh held back. He wasn't sure what to do. The three of them had been friends since third grade when they'd all moved to the neighborhood.

His mother had tried to get him interested in developing friendships with other kids, especially those in the church, but Josh had always fought it. Until now, their relationship had been clean and clear of major problems. Once Cam had gotten into trouble with a BB gun. And since he had his driver's license, they'd had more than one joyride out on Route 34. But he never thought something like this would come into their relationship. He'd known drugs were in the school. But the three of them had always stayed clear.

Cam's voice rang out over the parking lot. "You coming, Mr. Perfect Christian, or are you walking home?"

It was over five miles. But Josh didn't like the idea of driving in the car knowing there were drugs in it. He could call his mom. She'd be home.

Cam called out again. "Hey, Mr. Chicken, what are you—white meat or dark meat?"

Josh felt the anger shooting through his belly. Whenever Cam didn't get his way, he always became insulting. That was the one thing he'd never liked about Cam. Still, they'd been friends for years. Should he divide with them over something like this?

Josh pushed his feet in the direction of the car.

When he jumped into the back seat, a small baggie plunked into his lap.

123

"Take a look at it, jerko," said Cam. "See if it looks like it has a demon in it."

Jim said, "Come on, Cam, lay off. Josh needs a little time, that's all."

Cam started the engine and gave Jim a hard look. "Don't you go preachin' at me, or I'll lay you in the dust, boy."

Jim shook his head and shut up.

Josh looked at the baggie curiously. The marijuana looked like ground-up grass to him, or some kind of spice he'd seen in his mother's kitchen. He thought momentarily about throwing the baggie out the window. But he simply handed it back to Jim. "I said I'm not interested."

Cam threw the Chevy into gear.

Grazing

Often, when one ploy doesn't work, a person who wants you to do something will try another gambit. Remember the temptation of Jesus in Matthew 4? First Satan suggested that Jesus turn stones into bread. Jesus had fasted for forty days at that point. He would starve and die in a few more days if he wasn't careful. But he resisted, knowing that in order to obey the Father, he had to wait till the Father gave him the okay on food.

But Satan didn't sashay off and say, "Nice try, kid. Better luck next time." No, he immediately whipped out his second trick. He took Jesus into Jerusalem, had him stand on one of the high towers of the temple, and challenged him to jump off. Then he quoted a scripture that supposedly promised God would save him at the last moment. Why did Satan use Scripture? Because that's how Jesus defeated him on the first attack. It was as though Satan said, "So you're going to quote Scripture? Well, I can do that too."

124

Still, Jesus didn't give in, and found another scripture that spoke the truth.

Nonetheless, Satan still didn't give up. The next time, he pulled out the biggest ploy ever. He took Jesus to a high mountain and showed him the whole world "in a moment of time"—all its kingdoms and glory. Then he promised to give it all to Jesus if Jesus would just fall down and worship him. Of course, Jesus had another verse and dismissed Satan entirely.

The point is that some folks, when they don't succeed with us, they'll "try, try again."

When I went to parties as a teenager, my friends often got drunk. I remember one scene shortly after I became a Christian. I refused to drink. All my friends lined up to have their say in telling me off and why I was such a jerk.

A year after that, one of my friends in that group also became a Christian. He told me that he didn't understand himself at that time. "It was like we had to prove you were wrong about drinking to justify ourselves," he told me. "We were all outraged. Maybe, deep down, we all felt a little guilty."

I don't know the answer to that one, but I do know it's possible to keep resisting. It may be tough. It may win you rejection and even scorn. But you will have pleased the only one whom you have to please: Jesus.

Chew for Thought

1. What is the word of God designed to do? Why do Christians turn to it in their hour of need? Read about the purpose of God's word in the following places: Psalm 119:105, 1 Corinthians 10:11-12, 2 Timothy 3:16-17. What do they reveal to you that may help in time of need? _____

_____

_____

2. Do you have a favorite passage of Scripture that gives you strength? What is it? Why does it offer you strength and hope?_____

_____

_____

THURSDAY

A Secret

When he was alone that night, Josh sat in his room trying to sort things out. He'd heard all kinds of preaching against drugs. His father regularly gave lectures about it to him and his two sisters. But he'd always been able to say he wasn't interested in such things, and anyway he didn't hang around with kids who were. Now he was curious.

He picked up his Bible and leafed through it, but he didn't know where to turn or look for guidance. Really, he didn't think he needed any. He knew it wasn't right to take drugs, marijuana or otherwise.

Just the same, he didn't want to reject Cam and Jim and just go his own way. But he also knew this wouldn't be the end of it. Cam would be at him, trying to get him to try it. If they were to be friends, he had to make some things clear. But what?

On Saturday, Callie Abrams threw a going-back-to-school party. Josh was invited, and he knew Jim and Cam would probably be there. But he was sure they wouldn't mention the marijuana. Not at a party.

That night, Josh joined into the games and singing enthusiastically. Jim and Cam were there with some girls he didn't know, but they seemed to be having a good time. Several of the guys were in a band and had set up their equipment to play. They weren't bad, even doing a decent rendition of songs by U2, R.E.M., and 10,000 Maniacs. But gradually, the party began to break up into little groups. Josh knew some of them had gone around to the side of the house to do some drinking.

Suddenly, Beverly Pindale was at his arm. He'd always

127

liked her, but they'd never dated.

"Josh, would you come with me for a minute?"

She put her arm in his and snuggled closely to him. He hadn't counted on something like this.

"Where to?" he said.

"A secret," she said. He loved her smile.

She led him out of the room. He hadn't seen Callie's parents around, or any adults for that matter, and wondered about it briefly. Moments later she opened a door in a room upstairs. Smoke and a strange smell sifted out into the hall.

Grazing

Now Cam has others involved in his dirty work. That's the way peer pressure goes. Plenty of people can get involved. In one sense, they're doing it because they may even believe it's a good thing. They don't want you to miss something they think is exciting and fun.

One thing about sin that people are getting involved in: they want to spread it. Why? Because there's safety in numbers. How many times have you found yourself justifying something you know is wrong scripturally, but because so-and-so does it, you feel better about doing it yourself? We all spend long hours arguing against our parents and everyone else. And our parents aren't even there. We simply imagine what they'd say and then we knock it down. We give voice to our complaints and positions and always come out the winners. In effect, we try to justify what we know is wrong conduct. To ourselves. And to one another.

But numbers don't change anything. Even if the whole world goes the wrong way, God's way is still right. And the one who goes his way will be blessed—by God himself.

Chew for Thought

1. Look at a person who justified sin: King Saul in 1 Samuel 13:1-14 and 1 Samuel 15:1-31. What do you think of Saul's arguments? Why do you think they didn't hold water?_____

_____

_____

2. Are there sins you're trying to justify? What are they? Are you convinced you're right? Why or why not?

_____

_____

_____

FRIDAY

It Feels Great!

Josh spotted Cam and Jim immediately. There were also three girls and a guy with a spike haircut that he didn't know. Beverly clutched his arm. Immediately, Josh felt his forehead get hot, and he wanted to throw up.

"Hey, golden boy," said Cam. "You're just in time."

One of the girls said, "We hear it's your first time."

Josh tried to smile. He looked at Cam helplessly, then at Jim.

Beverly cooed into his ear, "I tried it for the first time a week ago. It was the biggest thrill."

Josh felt his chest pounding, and he looked at the door. It was already closed. The light was dim and the smokiness of the room made him feel dizzy. His mind groped through angry, hopeless thoughts. Everyone was looking at him.

"He looks paranoid already," said the guy with the spike haircut, "and he isn't even high."

"You just drag on the joint like a cigarette," said Cam, handing what looked like a hand-rolled cigarette to Josh. "Then hold it as long as you can. That's it."

Josh took the cigarette without even thinking. He felt like he was in a dream. All the smoke was making him feel dizzy. And he couldn't seem to think of anything to say.

"Go ahead," Beverly whispered into his ear. "It's tremendous stuff. Cam says he got it over at State."

Josh gazed around at the faces in the room. They all seemed blurry. Everyone was smiling. He felt dizzy. He put his left hand up to his forehead. "I feel sick," he said.

"Then take a puff," said Cam, his voice twinged with sarcasm. "It'll make you feel a lot better."

Josh closed his eyes. Suddenly, it was in his mind to pray.

Grazing

Unfortunately, when resisting peer pressure we often have to say no to the very people we most want to say yes to—our best friends. That's why it's so important to have friends with Christian convictions and beliefs.

A verse that has helped me in this matter is one often used in reference to dating, 2 Corinthians 6:14. "Do not be bound together with unbelievers; for what partnership have righteousness and lawlessness, or what fellowship has light with darkness?"

We need to be careful about what friends we choose to relate to. Choosing the wrong ones may have consequences for the rest of our lives.

If you know someone well enough, you are probably aware of what motivates him or her, what turns him or her on, where his or her weak points are. People who want to influence you for bad know just where to point the gun so that you throw your hands up and give in. We all know what can get to one another, don't we?

Chew for Thought

1. If you're unsure about what kinds of sins Scripture speaks against, read the following passages: Exodus 20:2-17, Mark 7:20-22, 2 Timothy 3:1-7, Romans 1:18-32, Galatians 5:19-21._____

_____

_____

2. Do you see anything in those lists that convicts you? If so, confess it. _____

_____

_____

WEEKEND

Help Me, Lord!

All Josh could think to pray was, "Help me, Lord." Then he looked at the red-tipped cigarette in his hand.

"Come on," said one of the girls, "he's wasting it."

Josh breathed out heavily. He knew he didn't want to get high, or smoke, or even be in that room.

"Maybe if he sits down," said Beverly. She began pushing him over to the bed.

"No!" said Josh, suddenly angry. "No!"

He glanced around and spotted what looked like a bathroom. With a sudden internal push of resolve, he began walking towards it.

"Hey, where're you going?" said Cam with exasperation.

Josh didn't answer. When he got to the bathroom, he quickly found the light switch, lifted the toilet seat, and threw in the lit joint. It hissed briefly. Then he flushed the toilet. Cam was already at the door. "Hey, jerko, what are you doing? That stuff's expensive." He pushed past Josh and looked at the swirling water. He swore and turned to grab Josh.

But Josh was already walking out.

Cam called to him from the bathroom door. "Hey, jerko, that joint cost five bucks."

Josh turned to look at him. He felt disgusted, angry, and afraid that he'd almost listened to them. He thought of several sarcastic things to say. But he simply said, "I don't care what you say, it's not right—for me, you, or anyone else. Now you do what you want. I'm leaving."

When he got to the door, he turned around and looked

at the group. The girls appeared embarrassed, Jim was staring at him, and Cam looked furious. The only one who was laughing was the spikehead.

Josh opened the door. Somehow he knew the best thing was just to get out of the house. He closed the door behind him, hurried down the stairs and out into the night.

When he reached his car, he breathed a sigh of relief and hopped in. As he drove home, he felt like cursing and then crying. Something in him told him this might be the end of his close friendship with both Cam and Jim.

Grazing

Josh realized an important truth: Just because people are urging you to do something doesn't mean you have to. No one can force you to do something you don't want to. It's up to you to decide what matters in life and what doesn't. Do things such as drugs, drinking, sex, and skipping school matter to you? Are they issues of high importance that you've already decided you're going to avoid—at all costs? Moreover, is having a pure, holy life before the Lord important? Does serving and pleasing him count? These are the real issues behind peer pressure. What you believe will determine how you handle that pressure.

Perhaps you saw the movie *Chariots of Fire*. It was about the 1924 Olympics. A young champion named Eric Liddell had stunned England and the world by refusing to run his best event, the one hundred meters, because the trial heats were run on a Sunday. He was a Christian. He believed fervently that he had to keep the fourth commandment, to remember the Sabbath and keep it holy. Great peer pressure was brought upon him, including a talk by the Prince of Wales. Many of his friends didn't understand and expressed their disagreement. But he didn't give in. He agreed to run in some other events, including the four hundred meters. It's a grueling race. A dash like the hundred meters, but long distance like the mile. All out for four hundred meters, two hundred paces. Your chest heaves. Your whole body begins to erupt.

Eric Liddell came to that moment. Perhaps he wondered if it had all been worth it, forfeiting his best event because he wouldn't run on a Sunday. But he had his beliefs. He had refused to give in to the pressure to run—but had he been right?

Then the gun roared and he fired forth, pressing every ounce of muscle and strength towards that tape. But Eric Liddell had an ally on his side, something no one else had in that race. It was a precious truth. The athletics masseur who attended to the British team had found a special heart in Eric. It had come out of his valiant desire to honor God. The masseur wrote him a note before he went to the line that day. It said, "In the old book it says, 'He that honors Me I will honor.' Wishing you the best of success always."

The gun resounded. Liddell bounded forth.

And he won.

Perhaps you feel the pressure's too great, your friends are making it too difficult, you have to give in. But don't. He who honors God, God will honor.

Chew for Thought

1. Do you find facing your fear in the midst of pressure a hard thing? Perhaps a few other words from God will help: Isaiah 40:27-31, Isaiah 43:1-3, Matthew 10:24-31. Anything stand out? What? Why? _____

_____

_____

2. Perhaps this week you have been convicted of behaviors your friends are trying to convince you to engage in.

135

If so, what do you believe God wants you to do? Will you do it?_____

_____

_____

WEEK SEVEN

My Back to the Barbed Wire

MONDAY

The Devil Gets an Opportunity

Among the artifacts discovered in the recent excavations at The Pit was the following correspondence from Scrubdub, a demon, to his disciple, Loopole.

Dear Loopole:

Your astonishment is revealing, my child. I told you our lawyers and agents, even Lucifer himself, are continually demanding opportunity to test a Christian to show his or her true self. Your lawyer won this occasion for you after years of proofs, briefs, indictments, and arguings. So it is with all saints. We repeatedly assert to the Enemy that if he'll let down his wretched hedge (remember my earlier letter about the hedge he places about all his children?) and give us a chance to assault freely, we'll prove once and for all that every one of them is a clod deserving just and final committal to our sphere.

If you look again into The Book, you'll see several occasions on which Our Father Below asked and gained permission to "sift" a man. Job is a good example. Lucifer even won an opportunity against the Son of God himself in the wilderness. As you know he was so befuddled by our Magnificent Lord that he resorted to that banal tactic of Scripture-prattling and quacking Bible quotes like a lame duck. Though our Lord was prepared, the son tricked him into departing by using the old "Begone, Satan" ploy, and, as you know, Lucifer hates that name. He decided at the time that if the son was going to resort to name-calling to push him off, then he'd have nothing to do with him.

You've been given a real opportunity with Jenkins. You must make the most of it. Don't be bothered that the Enemy has placed several limitations on you—that you can't harm him physically, that the duration of the test is dependent on the Enemy's will, and that you can't prevent the church from helping Jenkins. To be sure, the Enemy is unfair. What he gives with his right hand, he always takes back with his left. But if you think through what you will do, you shall not only have your man for breakfast and lunch, but also for supper and a mid-hell snack.

Scrubdub

Grazing

Testing. Just the word can strike fear into our souls. I still have bad dreams about tests in high school and college. I show up at the room, but it's the wrong room. Or I haven't studied the right subject. Or it's all in a language I can't understand. I wake up in a sweat.

But there is also the kind of testing the Bible speaks about. "Beloved, do not be surprised at the fiery ordeal among you, which comes upon you for your testing, as though some strange thing were happening to you; but to the degree that you share the sufferings of Christ, keep on rejoicing; so that also at the revelation of His glory, you may rejoice with exultation" (1 Peter 4:12-13). Christians will be tested in this life. Why? So that God can perfect us and make us more like Jesus.

But that doesn't make it easy.

A traveler in the Swiss Alps came upon such a shepherd weeping with a lamb in his lap. The lamb's leg was broken and the shepherd was trying to comfort it. The traveler's heart was moved and he asked how the break had happened. The shepherd said that he had broken the lamb's leg himself.

The traveler was aghast, but the shepherd explained, "This lamb is one of the most wayward in the whole flock. Every time I take the sheep out to graze, he leads others away from the flock and too close to the cliffs. He would wander with smaller lambs and get lost. I have to teach him to obey, and I'm doing it by breaking his leg. Until it heals, I'll carry him myself. And when he can walk again, he will be one of the most loyal and obedient lambs of all."

You will be tested. God will also work it so that you survive and emerge a stronger, more obedient person for it.

Chew for Thought

1. Read about Peter's test in Luke 22:31-34, 54-60. Why do you think God allowed this? How had Peter changed in Acts 2:14-16? _____

_____

_____

2. Do you think you're going through any tests at the moment? Why? Where do you see it all headed? Do you trust the Lord in this? Why or why not?_____

_____

_____

TUESDAY

Talking Strategy

Loopole:

I'm glad you asked. Strategy is important. How will we go about this little caper?

First, note that Jenkins has been thinking himself quite spiritual and mature of late. He was reported as recently musing that he'll soon be offered a position on the youth leadership council. This attitude is excellent, for it manifests pride. Pride always prevents a man from depending on the Enemy.

Second, you've properly planted a vague and caricatured image of us in his mind. It's always sensible to keep his mind on things of earth rather than the things above. As a result, he's not only unaware of the Enemy's presence, but he's also unaware of yours.

Now, how do you attack?

Remember several things:

1. *Subtlety.* Since he's underestimated you, he's also underestimated the subtlety of your attack. Thus, you want to plot out clearly what he'll be most unprepared for. For instance, I once destroyed a young man who was sports-oriented and highly competitive. He gave a vibrant testimony before various sports circles and was useful to the Enemy. But he began to love his testimony more than his Lord. He also began to think he was quite invincible and nontemptable. Then the Enemy gave us our opportunity. I was able to engineer a traffic accident and we sent the squeak into a truck. He ended up hospitalized and temporarily paralyzed. I had him carefully caulked into a state of blessed bitterness for months

and even hoped the lad would go the way of all agnosticism in the end.

2. *Surprise*. Don't mistake what I mean here. I'm not referring to the kind of attack that leaps out of the dark and pounces on him. What you want is for him to be bitterly disappointed. He must feel that the Enemy has let him down. He must think that everything he has believed is foolishness. He must become convinced that nothing in the Book works—the promises are vain, the commands are impossible, the stories ridiculous.

3. *The slow slide*. But again, don't get him going too fast. There's always the chance he'll jolt alert in the face of it. First you want disobedience to the Enemy's commands. Then distrust of the Enemy himself. Finally, the disowning of the Enemy.

Keep your head. Don't let him crack your nerve with Scripture-quoting. And don't be looking for the grand heist. Ease him down and you'll find he'll roast just as savory.

Scrubdub

Grazing

The devil has a strategy. He's working to make us ineffective for the kingdom of God. Are you aware of tricks he's used to try to lead you astray?

One of his best methods is referred to in 2 Corinthians 11:14: "And no wonder, for even Satan disguises himself as an angel of light." Satan doesn't want you to know you're being tested. He may drape the test in the finest garb possible. He'll come at you through your best friends (as we saw in the chapter on peer pressure), or he'll offer you fine promises if you'll just try this or that. "You'll feel better." "It's fun." Sometimes he'll try to shame you into sin. "You don't want your friends to think you're a geek." "You may not have another chance."

But you don't have to give in. Here's a word for the memory pad: "You are from God, little children, and have overcome them; because greater is He who is in you than he who is in the world."

The God of the universe, Jesus in the Spirit, dwells in all of us who name his name, love him, and believe in him. Do not fear. He is greater than all.

Chew for Thought

1. Can you think of a time when Satan deceived you? How did he do it? What did you learn from it?_____

_____

_____

2. What type of deception are you most susceptible to?

_____

_____

_____

WEDNESDAY

Bravo!

Loopole:

Even now I can taste Jenkins basted and broiled. Your strategy is brilliant. I've often used this tactic myself. Did you research this and happen upon my thesis on the use of depression in destroying saints?

Get Jenkins obsessed with the idea that if he can discover why all this is happening, he'll find an instant solution to the problem. We know he could never understand why in purely logical and human terms—the kind of terms he demands.

More importantly, the Enemy won't tell him why. (And I don't think you're planning on it, are you?) So by miring him in a quag of questions, you fix him in mental muck and aggravation that will keep him depressed for months to come.

Of course, you should offer Jenkins some fanciful explanations for his condition, such as, "You've committed some sin. If you could only find it and confess it, you'd be free." Or, "God is trying to teach you something. Once you learn the lesson, the trial will be over."

At the same time, I'd highly recommend reinforcing the idea that this condition will last the rest of his life. (Isn't it interesting the way a biped will, in one moment, believe the trial will never end, and in the next be praying fervently it will end that hour?)

Draw his attention to promises in Scripture (verses which he thinks are promises—not real promises such as "I will never desert you, nor will I ever forsake you"; but those he imagines are promises, like, "Ask and you shall receive"—

145

and, of course, remember to add the word *now* or *soon* or *within a matter of days* at the end).

You might lead him into another religion, at which time you can free him from his depression. Or you can simply bring him to the conclusion that Christianity is bunk and he'll have to find his own way in this world. Either way, you have your man.

Scrubdub

Grazing

A period of testing can involve many experiences. You might suffer from bad health, a disease, an emotional illness, paralysis, or a hospital stay. You might have a traffic accident, lose a close friend, move to another city, undergo rejection and persecution from others. The devil has many means at his disposal.

Jesus learned "obedience from the things which He suffered" (Hebrews 5:8). "It is for discipline that you endure; God deals with you as with sons; for what son is there whom his father does not discipline?" (Hebrews 12:7). "For to you it has been granted for Christ's sake, not only to believe in Him, but also to suffer for His sake" (Philippians 1:29).

For all of us, a time of testing is a "moment" to excel, to show what we're really made of inside.

It was February 22, 1980. Lake Placid, New York. The Winter Olympics.

The American hockey team was about to take on the Soviet storm skaters. Comparisons had been made. Everyone agreed. It was a little like a Little League team taking on the New York Yankees. The Americans win? Not a chance.

Enter Coach Herb Brooks. He'd taken those committed young men and brought them to the brink of immortality. Now they had to face the unbeaten Soviets. Perhaps he simply wanted to give them a shimmer of hope. He looked at his watch. 5 P.M. In moments they'd be in the rink, on their way to triumph, or just one more crunch-up for the Soviets. Brooks spoke quietly. "Don't be awed. The Russians are over-confident, ripe to be taken."

He let it sink in. "Stay with the system, dance with the girl that brung yah."

He waited. After a long pause, he pulled a scrap of paper from his pocket. He read to a hushed room. "You are born to be a player. You are meant to be here at this time."

Again, a pause. Then, "This is your moment."

Coach Brooks knew his players were being tested to the limits. But somewhere in the back of his mind, he must have seen beyond it all. This was their moment to show what they were made of.[1]

Similarly, testing is the Christian's moment to show his faith in a mighty God who will help us through everything.

Chew for Thought

1. Read more on the purpose of testing in Hebrews 12:1-13. What does this passage say about testing that sticks out in your mind?_____

_____

_____

2. Identify a time when your faith was tested. What happened? What did this test show you about the strength of your faith? _____

_____

_____

THURSDAY

Some Quibbling

Loopole:

This is no time for quibbling. You haven't got your man. He isn't dead yet, is he? It's only after a person has died unrepentant and faithless that he's secure.

Simply that Jenkins is questioning his faith in ways never before witnessed is no cause for feasting. The Enemy is allowing you to put him through a period of suffering.

If not properly directed by you, this could lead to refining and spiritual transformation that you will shudder to sniff.

To be sure, Jenkins is wondering why this is happening. He has long conceived of the Enemy as one who always gives joy, peace, and hope in circumstances. But this period of emotional turmoil has rocked his faith, or so he thinks.

What had you been telling him? That all will be well if he just trusts the Enemy? That nothing ever goes wrong in true Christians' lives? That all he must do is pray?

That was good as far as it goes. But the reason that we plant such ideas in our subjects is to head off precisely what is happening now. That is, if we get a biped to believe the above things, when calamity strikes he'll often give up the faith.

However, it can also go the other way. The Enemy can use a trial to screen out the theological gunk we've crammed into the subject's cranium. The result is a cleaner, more committed disciple than ever.

How then can you combat this possibility?

Jenkins is living with several important misconceptions

which you must keep advancing.

He thinks first of all that simply practicing spiritual disciplines insures that he'll always be happy, fruitful, and close to the Enemy. The result is that he's come to trust in his spiritual disciplines more than in the Enemy himself.

Second, he feels useless—he's not sharing his faith consistently, not participating in his class, not leading people to Christ—he feels that somehow he has failed the Enemy. Little does he know that the Enemy often renders his disciples ineffective (in the sense of not accomplishing many visible, tangible things for his kingdom) in order to draw them closer to himself and perfect them through suffering. This ultimately yields a more effective disciple. But you must keep Jenkins from realizing this.

Scrubdub

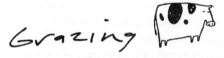

Grazing

Misconceptions about God's kingdom and truth are what fell more Christians than anything else. We come to believe something that is not scriptural (but which we may think is scriptural), we stake our faith on that falsehood, and when it fails, we blame God, or the Bible, or Christianity, or the church.

Some of those falsehoods that Christians believe today, but which are not true, are:

- God wants us always healthy; if we're not healthy, we must be sinning (see 2 Timothy 4:20, 2 Corinthians 12:9-10).
- God wants us successful and prosperous (see Revelation 2:8-11).
- God wants us to be happy above all (see Matthew 5:1-11).

- ◆ Christianity gets easier as you get older (see Romans 7:15-25).
- ◆ Bad things don't happen to Christians (see Acts 16:19-34).
- ◆ I've got Jesus, I'm going to heaven, so I can live like I want (see 1 John 2:4-6).

There are a multitude of such misconceptions that can waylay even the strongest saint. They lead us right into the pit.

If you're going through a test, your first source of wisdom is Scripture. But make sure what you think it's saying is what it really says.

One of the hardest misconceptions to dislodge from the average Christian's mind is that the Lord wants us happy, things to go well, and us to succeed in the primary situations of life. We believe that God can do anything, and therefore he will. A result of this misconception is that we often spend much of our time being discouraged and disillusioned.

There's a verse that has always helped me in this. It's Isaiah 55:8-9: " 'For My thoughts are not your thoughts, neither are your ways My ways,' declares the LORD. 'For as the heavens are higher than the earth, so are My ways higher than your ways, and My thoughts than your thoughts.'"

We always want things to work out, to succeed, to be happy, to have a glorious ending. But God doesn't always work that way. To be sure, in the end we will see the glory of it all. But that end does not occur till after Jesus has reigned for a thousand years. We've a long way to go before we reach it.

Chew for Thought

1. If you haven't already done so, look up the references that refute the misconceptions listed above.

2. What misconceptions do you have? Do you know what Scripture says on that issue? Why is your misconception a misconception?_____

_____

_____

FRIDAY

An Appalling Situation

Loopole:

Your last letter appalls me, and I can see the situation has gone beyond your control without your even realizing it. I thought you were ready for this, but now I'm not sure. Our negotiations with the Enemy specified that only you could attack Jenkins.

Here are your greatest errors.

You say (in some of the purplest terms I've seen from any demon), "The woolly haired tweet has been poring over the Scriptures and other books steadily in search of 'the deep dark secret verse'—HA!—that will zap him out of his circumstances. Little does he know there isn't a secret verse—HA HA!"

You have missed the point. So there isn't a secret verse? So he hopes there is? So he'll be disappointed when he fails to find it? You fool! He's reading his Bible like a gulag prisoner looking for slivers of meat! He goes to it every day full of anticipation and hope. Don't you see that even though at the end of the day he's discouraged and limp, he's learning what the Book says? Have you gone insane?

He's meditating on it, eating it, digesting it, grasping and grabbing and scrabbling and racing through it in search of something, anything to get him out of his depression. He cares nothing for magazines, tomes, digests, how-to books, or any other paraphernalia. He's actually become convinced that the Book alone has the answer! Get him reading *Sports Illustrated*, "Batman," a self-help book—anything but the Bible.

You make the same mistake with prayer. You say, "He goes to the Enemy daily, pleading, moaning, threatening, begging for relief, for an end. It borders on hilarity."

It grieves my hate to think that you revel in this.

Did it ever occur to you that though he's not praying much for others, and though his prayers have become a bit self-centered, the fact of the matter is that he is praying.

Furthermore, he's learning fervency in prayer, desperation, fire. He's no longer trying to win the world. He just wants to make it through one more day and not desert his Lord.

Do you see the horror of this? The Enemy has become his only hope, you dolt!

He's begun to see the Enemy as the first one to go to with a need, and the only one to go to. He's realizing that without the Enemy, he's nothing.

I had to fight last week to keep you on the case. There are demons in high places who want your throat, Loopole. Wise up, demon.

Scrubdub

Grazing

Spiritual disciplines—Bible study, prayer, Bible memory and meditation, witnessing, using your spiritual gifts, worship—are not an end in themselves, but a means to that end.

What then is our end? What are we seeking?

"Call to Me, and I will answer you, and I will tell you great and mighty things, which you do not know" (Jeremiah 33:3).

"Whether, then, you eat or drink or whatever you do, do all to the glory of God" (1 Corinthians 10:31).

"Come to Me, all who are weary and heavy-laden, and I will give you rest" (Matthew 11:28).

"I count all things to be loss in view of the surpassing

value of knowing Christ Jesus my Lord" (Philippians 3:8).

Jesus is our goal, our passion, our all-encompassing vision. The only way we can know him is by coming to him, walking with him, talking to him, and being in his presence. We learn of him through the Bible, other Christians, the church, prayer, applying his truth in the circumstances and tests of life. All of life is his lab, our hearts are his instruments.

Chew for Thought

1. Read about another who went through a severe trial of thinking all was lost but discovered it wasn't—Thomas, in John 20:24-29. What about Thomas's trial can you identify with? Why?_____

_____

_____

2. Do you see Jesus as your only hope in this world? Why or why not?_____

_____

_____

You've Lost Your Man

Loopole:

The man is "resigned to his condition"? Resigned? Is that all? What you should've said is that Jenkins has submitted himself entirely to the Enemy's sovereignty.

Apparently, though you've been allowed to keep Jenkins in this condition for over a year with no visible change, he finally gave up fighting and told the Enemy that he'd obey, love, and serve him regardless of whether he ever blessed him again. I hear the man got down by his bed and wept. I've received a transcript of the whole wretched prayer.

In a word, you've lost your man, Loopole. He's learned true submission. It will not be long before he's seeking to obey everything in the Book. For that reason, I'll make this short. You're not to be cast into the pit. No, we have better uses for the likes of you. Actually, we're leaving you on the case. We'll let you witness every day the growth this young twerp is going to experience. You're going to find out what it's like to have to be around a true saint. Have a ball, my friend.

Scrubdub

Grazing

The goal of all testing is ultimately to bring us into submission to the Lord. Jesus "learned obedience from the things which He suffered."

Obedience. What a difficult word. And a difficult thing to do. But that ultimately is what our lives are all about: learning to obey the Lord in all things.

Helen Keller became famous the world over because though she was blind, deaf, and dumb, she was able to overcome these handicaps and learn to speak and communicate despite them. Anne Sullivan was the woman who took over Helen's care while she was young because her parents could do nothing with her. Anne turned out to be a great teacher, one who worked with her student until she reached worldwide fame as an example of the human spirit and desire to triumph despite difficulties.

But early in their work together Anne saw that it would be impossible to train Helen without one ingredient lodged in her mind. Anne wrote, "I saw clearly that it was useless to try to teach her language or anything else until she learned to obey me. I have thought about it a great deal, and the more I think, the more certain I am that obedience is the gateway through which knowledge, yes, and love, too, enter the mind of a child."[2]

That's where the Lord's taking us—to know, yes, and to love. But first, to obey.

Chew for Thought

1. You'll find some more thoughts on discipline in trials in Psalm 14ℂ 10, John 14:15, 1 John 2:3-6, Revelation 22:7 and 14. Why not pick out one verse and memorize it?

2. Spend some time asking God to deepen your trust in him. If you feel that your faith in God has slipped, why not pray the following prayer?

Lord, I can't change my condition. So I'm willing to accept it. Whatever you want me to do, I'll do, even if my pain never lifts. I'll obey you, worship you, follow you, and love you as long as I live. I know now that you are God. I cast myself at your feet and only ask you to give me the grace to keep on going. Thank you for hearing me.

Week 7 Notes

1. P. Michelmore, "Team America," *Reader's Digest*, August, 1980, pp. 7-10.

2. Joseph P. Lash, *Helen and Teacher* (N.Y.: Delacorte Press, 1980), p. 52.

WEEK EIGHT

No Bullabout Going the Distance

MONDAY

He Had Told Us It Would Be Bad

The seven of us gazed out to the right of the little island, two hundred yards distant. My worst fears were quickly confirmed. A vicious, whistling wind was whipping up two- and three-foot whitecaps, bigger than any of us had seen, except Kevin, of course, our robust, bearded guide.

He'd told us South Lake would be bad. The Boundary Waters of Minnesota were notorious for their changes of weather, rapacious insects, and gusty wind—both sudden and strong, and always a threat to canoers like us.

The lake leaped and bucked like an enraged moose. I glanced at Kevin and asked, "Well, what do we do now?" I faintly hoped he might call in a helicopter, or wave a magic wand toward the lake and dispel the whitecaps, or at the very least, stop and camp where we were, on the portage from Rat Lake. But I knew that was illegal—and Kevin was a stickler for rules.

Kevin just laughed. "Into the canoes, guys. We've lost enough time already."

The group stood there, gaping helplessly at the convulsing water. Finally, Kevin moved and I mechanically began to load the canoes. Something inside me urged, "Stall. Go slow. You can't handle water like that." But as the leader of the youth group, I had to try to look confident. I began joking about it.

Later I would learn that several motorboats sank on a nearby lake during this storm—and we were in canoes. But I didn't know enough then to say this weather was perilous for amateurs like us—three adults, a high school senior, a freshman, and two junior high students. But we had wanted to do some "stress camping" in the Boundary Waters. And we had to follow the orders of our amiable and hopelessly calm guide.

Kevin paired me with David, the freshman. Then he and the others paddled off in the becalmed lee of the island. They would soon get into the raging waters to its right to get to our campsite for the night. I dreaded the idea even of getting into the canoe and closed my eyes, hoping that when I opened them it would all be over.

Grazing

One of my professors used to tell us, "The Christian life is not a hundred-yard dash; it's a marathon." Perhaps I should have thought of those words as I stood on the edge of South Lake that grim August morning. None of us likes pain—gritting our teeth, toughing it out, giving it all we got and then some. Enduring takes more than a prayer and a song.

The writer to the Hebrews pictured it this way: "Since we have so great a cloud of witnesses surrounding us, let us also lay aside every encumbrance, and the sin which so easily entangles us, and let us run with endurance the race that is set before us, fixing our eyes on Jesus, the author and per-fecter of faith, who for the joy set before Him endured the cross, despising the shame, and has sat down at the right hand of the throne of God" (Hebrews 12:1-2).

"Let us run with endurance."

Is that the way you picture the Christian life? I remember those first days in August, 1972, when I had just converted to faith in Christ. He was so near. Life was rich. Every experience had a golden glow. Nothing troubled me. I knew peace was real. I knew Jesus was in charge of everything. I wasn't afraid of anyone.

But those feelings departed and I was left with the reality of persevering. Just like on South Lake. We'd come into the camp with flags flying. But now everyone was damp, the flags were tattered, and it looked like a total loss.

Give up and go home?

I thought about it, but where else could I go? I was in the middle of the wilderness. It was sink or paddle.

Chew for Thought

1. What is enduring in the Christian life all about to you? Do you see yourself as enduring—hanging tough, sticking with it? Why or why not?_____

_____

_____

2. What does it mean to "fix our eyes on Jesus"? How can you do this today? This week?_____

_____

_____

TUESDAY

I Didn't See How We Could Make It

I pushed the canoe off into the slapping waves and jumped in. Instantly, we were in it, like specks in a boiling pot! Already the wind was trying to blow us back into the shore. David and I began paddling desperately just to keep us going straight and out from the beach.

But we were still in the lee of the island. We hadn't even begun to face the real fury of the waves. Kevin and Jeff were far out in the crashing waters to our right. Brian and Jim and Jim's son were farther to our right, falling back. I told David to keep moving ahead and use the island while we had the chance.

But we'd gone as far as we could in the island's protection. We had to face the churning waters to the north.

I said, "Let's go," and we were into it with the full fury of the wind screaming into our faces.

Cold spray peppered my face as our canoe bobbed and reeled in the churning water. Suddenly, the wind tugged at our bow, heaving us around. From the rear position, I stroked until my wrists shook with tension.

The wind wouldn't let up and dragged the canoe left and right, sloshing water over the gunwales. To turn broadside to the wind meant loss of control, no progress, and a possible spill. We'd lose all the equipment and maybe not recover for hours. My heart drummed wildly. I felt as though I could hear it above the din of the wind.

But I noticed we were making progress. The canoe inched back into the correct position. I shouted at David as we sweated and worked together. "Paddle on the right! We've got to get straight into the wind."

But we were losing ground. Kevin was still out far in front of us, but Brian and Jim had fallen behind. I was afraid to look back. I began mumbling prayers under my breath. "Please calm the wind down, Lord. Please help me to move ahead. Please don't let us turn sideways."

I felt myself tightening. The tension in my arms was increasing. I didn't see how we could keep up.

Grazing

Ever get that feeling of "There's no way we can make it. Let's give up"?

For most of us it happens every day. Peter probably felt that way after he denied Jesus three times. Even after Jesus appeared to him in his resurrection body, Peter didn't believe. He went back to his fishing.

Peter had given up. Perhaps what Peter needed to do was go way back to an event that happened years earlier when many disciples also were deserting Jesus. Jesus had spoken some "hard sayings," many of the people didn't like it, and they left, never to return to following him again. It was then that Jesus turned to the twelve and asked, "You do not want to go away also, do you?"

It was then that Peter came through with an immortal human response, something all of us will come to in the long race of the Christian life. He said, "Lord, to whom shall we go? You have words of eternal life. And we have believed and have come to know that You are the Holy One of God" (John 6:68-69).

"To whom shall we go?"

Have you ever thought seriously of giving up being a Christian? If you're honest and you've been through some hard times, you probably have. Don't be ashamed. Read about any great saint of the faith, and you'll find people who gave up, rebelled, failed, and then repented and came back to

Christ. It's a reality we all deal with. It's part of learning to walk with Jesus.

Sooner or later you'll come to some climactic trial where you will seriously think about giving up everything. It's then that you need to ask, "To whom shall I go?"

If you're truly his, there is only one answer. Your own heart will resound it within you. "There's nowhere else to go, Lord. You're my only hope. You have the keys to eternal life."

Chew for thought

1. Maybe you're wondering at this point if a "real" Christian can lose his salvation. I don't believe that's possible. Here are a few verses to help: Philippians 1:6, Jude 24-25, Romans 8:38-39. What do these passages teach you?_____
_____
_____

2. Can you remember a time in your life when you didn't believe in Christ? What changed? Why? Where do you stand today?_____
_____
_____

This Is Impossible!

We'd been at it nearly fifteen minutes with no progress when I glanced behind me to see how much distance we'd covered. As I did, Brian's canoe turned sideways into the wind. It was afloat, but could easily swamp. He screamed orders to Jim in the bow. For the first time, they both appeared frantic.

I prayed for them, then ducked my head back into the wind, wondering what to do. I felt a little stronger. But whitecaps smacked the left gunwale of the canoe and rolled us right, almost pitching me out. I screamed at David to shift his weight.

The canoe kept coming around. There was no way we could do this. We had had it. I was dead tired. I looked back and noticed then that Brian and Jim had stopped and gone back to the beach. Their canoe was already pulled up.

I shouted at David to head in.

The canoe sped around and in a few minutes we knocked up against the rock-strewn beach. We looked out and spotted Kevin, far north, still fighting the waves with Jeff. He finally turned around and in a few minutes he was back with us on the beach.

"What's up?" Kevin asked, irrepressibly calm.

I explained. "We just can't do it, Kevin. I've never seen waves like this. There's no control. Even Brian had to give up."

I glanced at Brian. He shrugged, while several others clamored, "I'm soaked." "Let's wait it out." "This is impossible."

Kevin shook his head and said, "Okay, let's give it an hour." He trudged off into the woods on one of his usual solitary meditative jaunts.

Grazing

Sometimes there are setbacks in the Christian walk. For a moment, it looks as though all is lost. You've failed. The end has come. Why not just drop in your tracks and ask to die?

Listening to some Christian leaders today, you get the impression that no real Christian lives in defeat, dejection, or spiritual dilapidation. No, we're supposed to have victory. One mountaintop to the next. "You can straddle those valleys. Don't worry about a little bump in the road. Get up and go!"

But there are defeats, setbacks, failures, "total destructions," and wipeouts in the Christian life.

I like what Jesus said to Peter shortly before the famed disciple was to deny he even knew Jesus to servant girls. Jesus said in Luke 22:31-32, "Simon, Simon, behold, Satan has demanded permission to sift you like wheat; but I have prayed for you, that your faith may not fail; and you, when once you have turned again, strengthen your brothers."

Notice Jesus' words. "I have prayed for you, that your faith may not fail." What might not fail? You personally?

No, that "your faith" might not fail. That's a different perspective. What is faith? If anything, it's a fluid, life-involved thing, not something static and fixed. It's like the fire in a fireplace. There are times when it roars up, making plenty of smoke, burning wood to cinders, and heating everyone up. But then there are times when it settles down to a steady glow. There even may be moments when it's down to one coal that appears to be going out. But with a little air, some fresh fuel, a few more coals, and some determined work, that coal can flame up again, perhaps more vigorously than before.

That's faith. It has its ups and downs, its highs, lows, and in-betweens. We exist on many levels—physical, emotional, mental, spiritual. Faith touches and is touched by each of those elements.

If you find yourself thinking your faith is going out, maybe like myself and my friends on that canoe trip, you need to stop, get quiet, pray, rest, and let the Lord speak to your heart. The Christian life isn't all action; sometimes it's just standing, waiting, and hoping.

Chew for Thought

1. For an interesting illustration of this truth, read about David and his men in 1 Samuel 30, with particular attention to verse 24. Why do you think David saw the sharing of the goods like this? Had some of the soldiers' faith failed?_____

_____

_____

2. When is your must vulnerable time? When are you most ready to give up? Can you analyze why and try to take measures to prevent it in the future?_____

_____

____ _____

THURSDAY

Something from Scripture

We sacked out for what seemed only seconds when Kevin's cheerful voice jolted me conscious. "Up! Let's go. We've been here over an hour."

I listened to the unchanged wind riffle through the trees and noted that my whole frame was shaking from the damp clothing. Even in August, Minnesota was cold.

The group began rising and lazily putting together a ramshackle array of paddles, tools, packs, and clothing. Everyone balked at stepping into a canoe.

Kevin stared at us, silently observing our progress. Finally, he pulled out a map and showed us an alternate campsite, one closer than our originally scheduled destination. It was only one mile up the lake, on the south side. "Surely we can make it that far," he said, wiping his mouth on his sleeve.

I reminded him that three members of our party were barely in their teens. But Kevin just peered into our cheerless faces and said, "Okay, guys, I'm going to give you something from Scripture."

I wanted to say, "Jesus isn't going to calm the storm for us," but I kept my mouth shut. Why waste the energy? Still, I wasn't in the mood for a sermon.

Kevin began to read, "Philippians 4:13: 'I can do all things through Him who strengthens me.'" Then in matter-of-fact tones, he exhorted us, "That's it, men. Whenever you feel like giving up, just think of that verse and pray. Let's repeat it."

We mumbled through the words once or twice. Kevin shook his head. "More enthusiasm. Let's hear it."

We wheezed the verse with a little more volume.

Kevin shook his head.

Then strangely, something seemed to ignite within me and after several more repeats, I shouted the verse like some cheerleader. As the others stared at me, I shrugged. "It can't hurt."

We boarded the canoes and set off, this time to the south, behind the island and into the raging waters on its left.

As the other two canoes surged into the spray, I shouted to David to conserve his strength.

And then we were in it for the second time that day.

Grazing

It's amazing to me how the word of God can work. Hebrews 4:12 tells us that "the word of God is living and active and sharper than any two-edged sword, and piercing as far as the division of soul and spirit, of both joints and marrow, and able to judge the thoughts and intentions of the heart."

God has invested his word with power. At times you might not see it or feel it. It may even appear boring and foolish in the hands of the wrong user. But the Lord has made clear to us that it has his personal power embedded in it.

That's why even a simple verse like Philippians 4:13 in the story above could take on new meaning as we faced the power of the wind and waves. It's not the cheerleading element, or the fact that we might crank up some nice feelings at the moment. But it's the fact that the Spirit of God is speaking—Spirit to spirit, heart to heart—that can turn a dismal moment into a triumph.

I'm not saying all you need is a Bible verse for your problem and you'll automatically march off into the sunset with victory banners flying. Rather, it's simply that the right word spoken in the right situation at the right time has power.

Chew for Thought

1. Read in another place in Scripture where a word from God helped some people who were on the brink of giving up: Luke 24:13-35. What do you see was happening in the minds of these men?_____

_____

_____

2. Put yourself in the position of those men on the Emmaus road. How might you have felt? How would Jesus' appearance have affected you? How does reading about that experience affect you now?_____

_____

_____

FRIDAY

Anything to Drown Out the Voice

The water seemed as thick as wet cement. I pulled my paddle through it with desperate chuffs in my throat. Tension crept up my fingers to my wrists. The other two canoes were out in front of us now, making progress. But there would be no racing today. I just wanted to survive.

Suddenly, spray pelted my face. The canoe lurched left. I strained and felt myself losing control of the canoe. I was tiring quickly. I shouted at David to switch sides—both of us on the left side trying to move it right, back straight into the wind.

Without planning, I began huffing out a prayer in rhythm to the stroking. "God . . . don't let . . . me give up. . . . Keep us . . . going. . . . "

Somehow my aching arms continued to press the paddle through the water. The words *just one mile* went through my mind over and over.

But it looked like a hundred miles.

As we labored, the canoe slowly came around.

In my mind, I worked toward a point one hundred yards distant. Suddenly, a new strategy crept into my thinking. I began making tiny mental goals, using landmarks on the shore. "If I can just make it to the evergreen . . . to that rock . . . to that cut in the trees . . . then I'll be all right."

Each time I reached a goal a minor explosion went off in my head. "Okay, you made it. Now just one more time."

I began counting strokes between goals. "40 . . . 91 . . . 124." Meanwhile an inner voice seemed to scream, "Give up. Think of a warm sleeping bag. You'll never make it."

But I hummed, whistled, sang, prayed—anything to drown out the voice.

Grazing

Strangely enough, one of the people we most battle when caught in desperate circumstances is ourselves. That potent, appealing voice within us sounds so sensible and right when it tells us to give in, stop, rest, go to sleep, forget the task at hand. It can paint pictures in our minds that won't let go. It can muster reason beyond all our powers to fight. It can sound so sure and caring that we think it must be right.

A proverb comes to my mind in this regard, Proverbs 14:12: "There is a way which seems right to a man, but its end is the way of death." That voice that sounds so cool, calm, and collected, that tells us there's no point in going on so why not give up is the voice of death, or perhaps of the devil himself. Resisting his reasonable arguments can feel like pushing nails through your fingertips. But James reminded us that when we submit to God, we can resist the devil, and he'll flee from us (James 4:7).

Have you been battling that inner voice lately? The promise of Christ is that even though it's a struggle, he's in there praying for you and pulling for you too.

When General Douglas MacArthur left Corregidor—"the Rock"—in 1942, fleeing from the Japanese invasion, he spoke those immortal words, "I shall return." Lieutenant General Jonathan Wainwright was left as commanding officer. In the face of an overwhelming attack, diminishing supplies, and soldiers who were starving, he surrendered to the Japanese shortly thereafter. For the next three years Wainwright struggled to survive as a prisoner-of-war in Manchuria. Perhaps he also heard that inner voice that told him to give up.

When he was released in 1945, Wainwright was a broken man. Haggard, aged, he needed a cane to walk. His eyes had sunken deeply into his head. His hair was snow-white. Pits clustered his cheeks. When he first faced General

MacArthur, he couldn't speak. For all those years he imagined himself a disgrace because of his surrender. He believed he'd never get another command. MacArthur himself was shocked that Wainwright believed this. His first words to his former officer were, "Why, Jim, your old corps is yours when you want it."

At that moment, Wainwright's voice broke. He said, "General . . . ," and burst into tears.[1]

Perhaps you feel a failure because you've given up at times as a Christian. Stop. Your Lord says to you, "I am with you always, even to the end of the age."

Chew for Thought

1. What was it that kept Paul in the race of life? Read Romans 8:18 for an answer. Why do you think Paul focused so much on "the glory that is to be revealed to us"? What power does it have in your life?_____

_____

_____

2. If you're interested in seeing how Paul's life did turn out, read 2 Timothy 4:6-8. Why do you think Paul likens the Christian life to fighting the good fight, finishing the course, and keeping the faith? What do these three facets—fight, course, faith—suggest to you about Christian living and what is important?_____

_____

_____

WEEKEND

I Needed It!

The wind kept dragging our canoe off bearing. The other two canoes had passed us and were now out of sight. I knew we couldn't last much longer, but I goaded myself with sharp promises: "Just around the next point." "Just past that clump of trees."

Yet, as we passed these points, there was no campsite, no canoes pulled up on the shore. We'd been at it several hours. My chest felt ready to explode.

Suddenly, as my thoughts sank, the wind gusted and pitched us right. The spray whipped my face and stung. I screamed to David to paddle hard. He snarled back at me, "What do you think I'm doing?"

Rage at him, at me, at the wind, at God seared through me. I seethed out angry prayers, reminding God that if he was so powerful, why didn't he do something.

The canoe was turning and swamping. Waves slammed against the gunwales and sloshed onto the floor. Our jackets and pants were soaked.

For minutes we battled, both of us paddling on the right side, trying to pull the bow around. But we couldn't hold it.

I yelled at David to let it come around. Water rolled about on the bottom of the canoe.

David relaxed and the canoe bobbed around. As it jerked about, I bit my lip. I didn't want to give up. But my arms felt like barbells. In my mind I raced through several alternatives: rest on the shore and try again, walk the canoe through the water close to the shore, portage it through the woods.

Instantly, fury at everything scorched through me as I

watched the canoe speed by stumps and rocks that had served earlier as marks of progress.

The anger seemed to rise and immediately I began shouting, "We're not gonna give up. Give it all you got. Bring it around from the other side."

Moving that bow was like moving a stalled truck. The wind kept throwing us farther back, hurling frigid spray into our faces and wearing our resolve. Yet, somehow, inch by inch, the bow lugged around. Soon we were straight.

Then, just as suddenly, the wind tore us the other way.

I screamed above it in fury. David laughed. Then I laughed. "We're gonna do it. Hang in there."

We fought to keep the canoe straight. My arms stiff with tension, I forced the paddle through the water.

Then the canoe straightened and held.

Around the next point, we caught the others. Their canoes beached, we began heading in when Kevin told us to keep going. "We can't find the campsite. Don't come in. It'll be harder to get back out."

I wheezed a prayer. "Come on, Lord. We need your help."

We banged on for another thirty minutes.

Around another point, we reached the site. David shouted and I gritted my teeth, silencing an inner squeal of triumph. We still had a hundred yards to go.

And then we were there.

After beaching the canoe, David and I sprawled onto the ground, gasping. Incredibly, we both started to laugh. When the others reached us, I stumbled about, lightheaded and stiff, but grinning.

Soon, everyone was chattering about the wind and waves, the exhaustion, and the impossible notion that we'd made it. Kevin scrutinized the map. After a brief look, he beamed a huge smile and said, "We missed the first campsite. We've come over two miles. You guys are tough."

Grazing

If you're like me, you probably look at other Christians who seem to "have it so together" and think you'd never attain to the spirituality and maturity they have. It's so easy to put up a "front" and appear to be something you aren't.

If there's anything that's true of us Christians, it's this: we can't do it on our own. All of us, no matter how confident we appear on the surface, struggle with the same problems, negative impulses, fears, and difficulties. Some of us might look like we "have it all together." But if we knew the truth, we'd realize that no one in this life ever will. Apart from Christ, we can do nothing (John 15:5).

Have you thought seriously about giving up then? Let me encourage you with another story:

A man had a dream. He was told by God to split a giant granite rock. He was banging away at it with his pick, but nothing happened. Finally, after much effort, he stopped. "It's useless. I'll never break the rock."

Suddenly, a man stood by him in his dream. The man said, "Weren't you given a job to do? If so, why have you stopped?"

The worker replied, "The work is useless. I can't make any impression on the rock." The stranger then said, "What's that to you? Your duty is to bang away at the rock, whether it breaks or not. The work is yours. The results are in other hands. Therefore, work on."

In the dream, he sighed and hoisted the pick over his head. With one blow, the whole rock split cleanly.

You might think being a Christian is too hard or that it's taking too long to see results or perhaps that it just doesn't have the glamour that it once had. But remember that it doesn't always take just one whack at the rock; sometimes it takes a hundred. Or five hundred. But the great truth is that Jesus will be there swinging with you and through you.

Chew for Thought

1. For a final thought on what it means to walk with Christ, read Galatians 3:1-9, 5:2-7, and 6:9-16. What do you see here that speaks to your life and needs?_____

_____

_____

2. Think again about Paul's words in Galatians 6:9-10. What do they say to you personally?_____

_____

_____

Week 8 Notes
1. William Manchester, *American Caesar: Douglas MacArthur, 1880-1964* (New York: Dell Publishing Co., 1979), pp. 524-525.

BULL'S-EYE!

One of my professors used to say, "Has God ever hit you over the head with a two-by-four?"

In the context of this book, maybe we might phrase it, "Has God ever put one of his arrows in your bull's-eye?"

We've looked at a number of tough issues that many of us don't like to talk about. We'd rather pretend they weren't there. Or worse, we deal with them superficially, then run along on our way.

But that's not God's way.

If you've learned anything in these pages, I hope it's this: obey God. If you do, he will be pleased and you will be blessed. Maybe not the way you'd like, or the way you'd think. But you will grow and become a more mature Christian.

Believe me, I know how hard obedience is. I struggle with it about 168 hours a week. (Seven times twenty-four?) On second thought, better make that 10,080 *minutes* a week.

At any rate, it remains a struggle. But don't think Jesus doesn't understand how hard it is. Remember what he prayed in the garden of Gethsemane shortly before his crucifixion? "My Father, if it is possible, let this cup pass from Me" (Matthew 26:39). Jesus didn't find his final act of obedience any easier than you and I do.

Still, obedience is a key I've emphasized in these pages. The Christian life can be boiled down to one word: faith. Obedience is the result of all true faith. I hope it's the kind of faith you have.

Thus, I hope working through this book has been a life-transforming journey for you. It has for me.